We would like to dedicate

this book to Mandy, J.P., and Samantha Stainback

for their patience and support.

Integration of Students with Severe Handicaps into Regular Schools

Susan Stainback and William Stainback

A Product of the ERIC
Clearinghouse on Handicapped
and Gifted Children

The Council for Exceptional Children

Library of Congress Cataloging in Publication Data

Stainback, Susan Bray.
  Integration of students with severe handicaps into regular schools.

  "A product of the ERIC Clearinghouse on Handicapped and Gifted
Children, The Council for Exceptional Children."
  1. Handicapped children—Education—United States—Addresses, essays,
lectures. 2. Mainstreaming in education—United States—Addresses, essays,
lectures. I. Stainback, William C. II. Council for Exceptional Children. III.
ERIC Clearinghouse on Handicapped and Gifted Children. IV. Title.

LC4031.S83 1985   371.9'046   84-27439
ISBN 0-86586-151-X

A product of the ERIC Clearinghouse on Handicapped and Gifted Children.

Published in 1985 by The Council for Exceptional Children, 1920 Association
Drive, Reston, Virginia 22091-1589.

This publication was prepared with funding from the National
Institute of Education, U.S. Department of Education, under
contract no. 400-81-0031. Contractors undertaking such projects
under government sponsorship are encouraged to express freely their judgment
in professional and technical matters. Prior to publication the manuscript
was submitted to The Council for Exceptional Children for critical review
and determination of professional competence. This publication has met such
standards. Points of view, however, do not necessarily represent the official
view or opinions of either The Council for Exceptional Children, the National
Institute of Education, or the Department of Education.

Printed in the United States of America.

Contents

Contributors

Dianne Ferguson
Syracuse University
Syracuse, New York

Susan Hamre-Nietupski
University of Northern Iowa
Cedar Falls, Iowa

Janet Hill
Virginia Commonwealth
  University
Richmond, Virginia

Gloria Shizue Kishi
Windward Oahu School District
Kaneohi, Hawaii

Ralph J. McQuarter
University of Minnesota
Minneapolic, Minnesota

Luanna H. Meyer
Syracuse University
Syracuse, New York

John Nietupski
University of Northern Iowa
Cedar Falls, Iowa

Susan Stainback
University of Northern Iowa
Cedar Falls, Iowa

William Stainback
University of Northern Iowa
Cedar Falls, Iowa

Steven J. Taylor
Syracuse University
Syracuse, New York

Paul Wehman
Virginia Commonwealth
  University
Richmond, Virginia

A Special Note

This book was written to outline ways of promoting integration between students with severe handicaps and their peers within current school organizational structures, wherein students, teachers, administrators, and school programs are generally divided into two basic kinds—regular and special. It is our personal belief that the special/regular education dichotomy that now exists will one day be dissolved and that natural, normalized integration of all students, teachers, etc. will be much easier to accomplish than it is at the present time. (See our article, "A Rationale for the Merger of Special and Regular Education," in *Exception Children*, volume 51, number 2, pp. 102-111.) However, until that day occurs, "special" and "regular" educators will need to work together within the current structure of the schools to promote as much natural, normalized integration as possible of all students within regular neighborhood public schools. We hope that this book will be of some assistance to both "regular" and "special" educators in their efforts to promote integration.

Susan Stainback
William Stainback
August 16, 1984

Preface

The responsibilities of teachers in regard to the integration of students with mild handicapping conditions into regular school activities have increased dramatically during the past several decades. Currently, there is growing recognition that both regular and special class teachers also have responsibilities in regard to the integration of students who experience severe handicaps. Many school districts throughout the United States have begun the process of integrating these students into regular schools. While most of them are generally placed into self-contained special education classrooms, they are often integrated into as many regular school programs and activities as possible. Many of them are attending assembly programs, eating lunch, going to the rest room, and sharing many activities such as Thanksgiving and birthday parties, rest time, homeroom, art, music, and recess with their nonhandicapped peers.

Because the movement to integrate students with severe handicaps into regular schools is very recent, there is little information in books on mainstreaming about integrating these students into regular school programs and activities. To date, publications on mainstreaming have focused almost exclusively on the integration of students with mild handicapping conditions into regular classes. In contrast, this book focuses on the integration of students with severe handicaps into regular schools. The book was written because the support and cooperation of both regular and special classroom teachers is imperative if students with severe handicaps are to become integral members of regular schools.

This book, (although focused primarily toward classroom teachers) may also be of use to a wide array of people such as professors, researchers, administrators, and parents. It is designed to fit as a supplemental text in introductory courses for special education teachers preparing to teach students with severe handicaps. In addition, it could also be used for workshops or short courses for special and/or regular classroom teachers concerning practical ways of integrating students with severe handicaps into regular neighborhood public schools.

The text is divided into five sections. Section one includes two chapters. Chapter one provides an overview about students with severe handicaps. Chapter two provides background information on why students with severe handicaps are being integrated into regular schools and the role of regular and special class teachers in these integration efforts.

Section two includes three chapters. All three chapters focus on interactions in school settings between nonhandicapped students and students with severe handicapping conditions. The first chapter in section two (Chapter 3) outlines practical ways of providing nonhandicapped students with opportunities—during already existing school activities— to interact with students with severe handicaps. Chapter four provides a practical and easy to use checklist for assessing the opportunitiers students with severe handicaps have for interaction with their nonhandicapped peers in a variety of school settings. Chapter five includes a variety of procedures that can be used to promote positive interactions between students with severe handicaps and nonhandicapped students, when positive interactions do not develop spontaneously.

Section three contains three chapters. All three address a major concern in the integration of students with severe handicaps into regular schools, that is, educating nonhandicapped students about individual differences. The first chapter in section three (Chapter 6) provides a rationale for educating nonhandicapped students. Chapter seven includes methods for assessing nonhandicapped students' knowledge, attitudes, and behaviors toward students with severe handicaps. Chapter eight presents a training model for educating nonhandicapped students about individual differences.

Section four includes two chapters. Both of these chapters focus on training students with severe handicaps in social and other skill areas that will facilitate their integration and interaction with their peers and other community members. Chapter nine provides procedures to plan, program, monitor, and assess interaction/social skill training of students with severe handicaps. Chapter ten describes how nonhandicapped peer assistance can be utilized in enhancing the social as well as other skills of students with severe handicaps.

The last section, section five, provides additional information that could be useful to classroom teachers in promoting the positive integration of students with severe handicaps into regular school programs and activities. Chapter eleven provides teachers with a series of organizational arrangements and concerns that are needed in the preparation of a school for integration and the continued maintenance of a healthy environment to foster positive integration of students with severe handicaps. Chapter twelve includes information that could assist teachers in organizing for the integration of students with severe handicaps into non-school, community settings. Chapter thirteen is a summary and resource chapter that provides a description of strategies used in successful integration programs throughout the nation as well as a discussion of selected resource materials that could be used to facilitate the integration procedures discussed throughout the text.

We would like to acknowledge a number of people who made this book possible. First, we acknowledge the contributing authors, who responded to our request for various chapters in their respective areas of expertise with high quality material. We also would like to acknowledge Dr. Marlene Strathe, Associate Dean of the College of Education at the University of Northern Iowa, who provided encouragement and concrete support while we were writing/editing the book, and Ms. Ruth Petersen for the excellent typing assistance provided with an ever pleasant, cheerful attitude. Finally, we would like to acknowledge Dr. June Jordan who was instrumental in the Council for Exceptional Children publishing the book and who has always been positive and consistent in encouraging our professional efforts.

Section I

Background

Chapter 1

Who Are the Students of Concern?

There is a growing recognition that a new group of students is being integrated into neighborhood public schools. Who are these relatively newly recognized students for whom the regular public schools must now provide programs? The authors' purpose in this first chapter is to provide a brief overview of who these students are and some of the problems associated with trying to characterize and define them.

WHO ARE THEY?

Students who experience severe handicapping conditions include those who have traditionally been classified as seriously emotionally disturbed, autistic, schizophrenic, severely/profoundly mentally retarded and/or multiply handicapped. They are students who in the past were often excluded from regular schools, and who may have been placed in segregated special schools and/or large state institutions. They were excluded from regular neighborhood schools because they typically lacked skills such as (a) ambulation; (b) the ability to easily communicate their needs; and/or (c) self-care skills, particularly dressing, toileting, and independent eating. Other reasons for excluding them included the unusual medical problems of some and the deviant behavior they sometimes exhibit. In addition, it was felt by many professionals and parents (and still is in some cases) that the "specialized" services that these students sometimes need could best and most efficiently be delivered in settings other than regular neighborhood schools.

There have been attempts during the past decade to precisely define students who experience severe handicaps. One of the first widely recognized definitions was formulated in 1974 by The United States Office of Education (USOE), Bureau of Education for the Handicapped (now Office of Special Education and Rehabilitative Services).

Severely handicapped children are those who, because of the intensity of their physical, mental or emotional problems or a combination of such problems, need educational, social, psychological, and medical services beyond those which are traditionally offered by regular and special education programs, in order to maximize their full potential for useful and meaningful participation in society and for self-fulfillment. Such children include those classified as seriously emotionally disturbed (schizophrenic and autistic), profoundly and severely mentally retarded, and those with two or more serious handicapping conditions such as the mentally retarded-blind and the cerebral palsied-deaf.

Such severely handicapped children may possess severe language and/or perceptual cognitive deprivations and evidence a number of abnormal behaviors including: failure to attend to even the most pronounced social stimuli, self-mutilation, self-stimulation, manifestations of durable and intense temper tantrums, and the absence of even the most rudimentary forms of verbal control, and may also have an extremely fragile physiological condition. (USOE, 1974, section 121.2)

Most current definitions of students who experience severe handicaps are similar to the USOE definition. One major drawback to these types of definitions is that they tend to focus almost exclusively on the negative behavioral characteristics that such students *may* possess. Such definitions leave the reader with the impression that students called severely handicapped are so "abnormal" that it would be almost impossible for them to function in the mainstream of society. However, many educators, who have worked extensively with these students in public school settings, have found that this is not the case (e.g., Nietupski, Hamre-Nietupski, Schuetz, & Ockwood, 1980). While many of them possess one or more of the characteristics described above, they seldom possess a majority of them. In addition, they have many positive characteristics (e.g., warmth, sense of humor) in spite of their serious handicapping condition(s). Also, many students who experience severe handicaps are now mastering skills once thought almost impossible for them to learn (e.g., independent dressing, bus riding, cooking, and/or supermarket shopping). Somehow the positive characteristics of these students and what they can learn have been overlooked in many definitions. Recent attempts in regard to defining students who experience severe handicaps have been focused toward trying to formulate definitions that are more service oriented, positive, and educationally relevant (Sontag, Smith, & Sailor, 1977). However, at present there is no widely accepted definition that has replaced definitions such as the one given above (Geiger & Justen, 1983).

Before closing this section, it should be noted that the terminology used to refer to such students has changed over the years and continues to change as the knowledge base in special education expands and grows. In the past, they have been referred to as imbeciles, idiots, custodial cases, and/or trainable retardates. Currently, they are often referred to with terms such as severely/profoundly retarded, autistic, schizophrenic, or simply as "persons with severe handicaps." But, as with the definitions, there is no widely accepted and agreed upon terminology at this point in time.

PROBLEMS IN DEFINING STUDENTS
WHO EXPERIENCE SEVERE HANDICAPS

While many educators agree that a positive and educationally relevant definition is needed, there are several reasons why there has been difficulty in reaching consensus on a definition. For example, students who experience severe handicaps represent a heterogeneous group. As noted earlier, those who have been traditionally classified as autistic, schizophrenic, severely/profoundly mentally retarded, and/or multiply handicapped are included. Thus, descriptions of these students would probably vary in proportion to the numbers of professionals asked to describe them. Also as Haring, Nietupski, and Hamre-Nietupski (1976) have observed, the idea of a set of static characteristics that could be used to define this (or any) population of students is highly questionable. Recent educational programming with these students has demonstrated that their behavioral characteristics, like those of all students, can be modified. Thus, the state of being severely handicapped is a changing one; that is, a child could be considered severely handicapped at one point in his or her life and not severely handicapped at another point.

It should be noted that while many educators believe that an agreed upon definition is needed (e.g., Geiger & Justen, 1983), a growing number of professional educators are not sure that any type of definition is really necessary in order to serve students who experience severe handicaps effectively in public schools. Wilcox (1979) stated the following:

> While it is generally believed that the essential first step in developing services, programs, and curricula for a target population is to arrive at a precise written definition of that population, such an undertaking may be neither functional nor necessary in accomplishing the intent of education—to change student behavior. (p. 138)

She believes that problems associated with definitions have consumed enormous professional energy that might otherwise have been invested in direct service or in the development of improved instructional programs for all children, including those labeled severely handicapped. The authors of this book tend to agree with Wilcox.

CONCLUSION

Regardless of the current problems related to definition and terminology, it is clear that there is a new group of students who are being integrated into regular neighborhood schools. Probably, the most essential point to remember is that they are students in need of educational training, just like any other member of the student body. While they may display serious intellectual, physical, emotional, and/or social difficulties, experience has shown that this does not preclude their participation in many regular school programs and activities (Baumgart et al., 1982; Brown et al., 1979).

Finally, students with severe handicapping conditions have throughout history borne numerous pejorative, socially stereotyped, and educationally irrelevant labels. As noted in this chapter, they have been called idiots, imbeciles, psychotics, and cripples. They have been described as trainable, subtrainable, multihandicapped, autistic, schizophrenic, semi-independent, and retardates. The expectations attached to these labels have hardly been flattering or educationally relevant (Wilcox, 1979).

Fortunately, in recent years society's attitudes toward students who experience severe handicapping conditions have changed dramatically. No longer are educators content with merely defining and labeling this population of students. Educational programs are being developed and organized to help them capitalize on their learning potential. Few educators today focus discussions on what these students can *not* learn or what they can *not* do. Their attention is focused on what they *can* learn and what they *can* do.

In summary, we have begun to move from a largely negative orientation regarding students who experience severe handicapping conditions toward a positive one that stresses their potential and the design of educational programs for them. While much more needs to be done, many professionals believe that we are now headed in the right direction.

REFERENCES

Baumgart, D., Brown, L., Pumpian, I., Nisbet, J., Ford, A., Sweet, M., Messina, R., & Schroeder, J. (1982). Principle of partial participation and individualized adaptations in educational programs for severely handicapped students. *The Journal of the Association for the Severely Handicapped, 7,* 17-27.

Brown, L., Branston, M., Baumgart, D., Vincent, L., Falvey, M., & Schroeder, J. (1979). Utilizing the characteristics of a variety of current and subsequent least restrictive environments as factors in the development of curricular content for severely handicapped students. *AAESPH Review, 4,* 407-424.

Geiger, W., & Justen, J. (1983). Definitions of severely handicapped and requirements for teacher certification: A survey of state departments of education. *The Journal of the Association for the Severely Handicapped, 8,* 25-30.

Haring, N., Nietupski, J., & Hamre-Nietupski, S. (1976). *Guidelines for effective intervention with the severely handicapped: Toward independent functioning.* Unpublished manuscript, University of Washington, Seattle.

Nietupski, J., Hamre-Nietupski, S., Schuetz, G., & Ockwood, L. (Eds.) (1980). *Severely handicapped students in regular schools.* Milwaukee: Milwaukee Public Schools.

Sontag, E., Smith, J., & Sailor, W. (1977). The severely and profoundly handicapped: Who are they? *Journal of Special Education*, *11*, 5-17.

United States Office of Education. Definition of severely handicapped children. Code of Federal Regulations, 1974, Title 45, Section 121.2.

Wilcox, B. (1979). Severe/profound handicapping conditions. In M.S. Lilly (Ed.), *Children with exceptional needs*. New York: Holt, Rinehart and Winston.

Chapter 2

Rationale for Integration and the Role of Special and Regular Classroom Teachers

As noted in the preface to this book, students with severe handicaps are being integrated into regular school programs throughout the nation. They are riding school buses, attending assembly programs, eating lunch, going to the restroom and sharing many activities such as art, music, and recess with their nonhandicapped peers (Brady & Dennis, 1984).

The authors' have three purposes in this chapter. The first is to outline why students with severe handicaps are being integrated into regular schools. The second is to discuss the benefits of integration to both nonhandicapped students and students with severe handicaps. The third is to discuss the special and regular classroom teachers' role in the integration of students with severe handicaps into regular schools.

REASONS FOR INTEGRATION

 There has been a gradual progression over the years toward increased integration into the mainstream of education of all individuals experiencing handicaps. As Reynolds and Birch (1977) stated: "The whole history of education for exceptional children can be told in terms of one steady trend that can be described as progressive inclusion" (p. 22). This progression, which can be traced back to as early as the 1700's (Stainback & Stainback, 1980), has in recent years gained pronounced momentum. The formulation and wide acceptance by human service professionals of the "normalization principle" helped to propel the integration movement, especially for persons with severe handicaps. Nirje (1969) phrased the principle as ". . . making available to severely retarded (or handicapped) persons patterns and conditions of everyday life which are as close as possible to the norms and patterns of the mainstream of society" (p. 181).

Litigation and legislation in the 1970's established the right of students with severe handicaps to a free and appropriate education. This reinforced the concept that persons with severe handicaps are integral members of society, who not only should be afforded but have a basic right to normalized life styles. In 1971, the *Pennsylvania Association for Retarded Children v. Commonwealth of Pennsylvania* court decision acknowledged the rights of students with severe handicaps to a free public education. Further litigation at both the state and national levels has continued to uphold this position.

Because of the growing national concern for the education of all children experiencing handicaps, in 1975 the Congress of the United States passed Public Law 94-142, mandating a free and appropriate education for all students with handicaps in the *least restrictive environment* (LRE). While this law has been cited repeatedly to support the rights of students with mild handicaps to be educated in the LRE, it should be noted that the law also addresses the rights of students with severe handicaps to be educated in the LRE. This law, The Education of All Handicapped Children Act, provided implementation power and incentive for educators to begin seriously addressing the needs of students with severe handicaps in the most normalized environments possible. Since this legislation, experience has shown that educational services can be successfully provided to students with severe handicaps within regular community public schools (Hamre-Nietupski & Nietupski, 1981). In addition, researchers have found that both students with severe handicaps and nonhandicapped students who share well-supervised interaction experiences in integrated situations can benefit educationally and socially from such experiences with no detrimental effects for either group (Stainback & Stainback, 1981).

Based on experience and research evidence, many professional educators have recently accepted the position that the least restrictive educational environment for students with severe handicaps is the regular neighborhood public school. This is evidenced in part by the fact that in 1979, The Association for Persons with Severe Handicaps (TASH) adopted a resolution calling for the education of all students with severe handicaps in regular public schools with their nonhandicapped peers. Recently, the National Society for Children and Adults with Autism adopted a similar resolution calling for the termination of segregated placements and encouraging integrated placements.

BENEFITS TO NONHANDICAPPED STUDENTS*

The public school experience should prepare all students for the realities of after-school and postschool life. Increasingly, students with severe handicaps will function in the wide variety of nonschool

---

*The material in this and the following section has been adapted with permission from Brown, Ford, Nisbet, Sweet, Donnellan, and Gruenewald (1983).

environments frequented by nonhandicapped persons who must now learn to interact with and to operate in their presence. Perhaps the reader has had the opportunity of taking a student with a severe handicap(s) to an environment that contained inexperienced nonhandicapped persons. The stares, fears, negative comments, and interruptions in routine would be minimized if opportunities to grow up and attend school with students who experienced severe handicaps had been provided. Additionally, if one examines some of the many roles and responsibilities assumed by nonhandicapped adults, the benefits of longitudinal and comprehensive interactions with severely handicapped persons can readily be discerned. Consider just three such benefits: education of future service providers, education of future parents, and development of perspective.

Future Service Providers

If a person is planning to become a nurse, when is the best time to learn about and to function with children who experience severe handicaps? In nursing school? After obtaining a job? Hardly. The best way for physicians, secretaries, group home managers, waiters, architects, nurses, teachers of nonhandicapped students, school board members, legislators, and others to develop the skills and attitudes necessary to function effectively for and with persons with severe handicaps is to grow up and attend school with them. We have tried it the other way, and it simply has not worked. Why is the turnover in group homes so high? Why do so many regular educators reject children with disabilities? Why do pediatricians still encourage parents to send their children to lives of waste and degradation in the wards of institutions? If they had grown up with peers who experienced severe handicaps, it is extremely doubtful that they would act in such negative, feudal, and rejecting ways.

Future Parents

Few persons with severe handicaps produce children with severe handicaps, yet by definition 1% of the children born every year will be intellectually severely handicapped. Who will produce these children with severe handicaps 5, 10, 15 years from now? Where are they now? What are they learning about their future children with severe handicaps? Nonhandicapped students who are currently functioning in regular schools are the future parents of children with severe handicaps. As educators we are remiss in our responsibilities if we do not provide them with the vitally needed preparatory experiences. Tragically, many of these parents are 30 to 35 years old and have never seen a person with a severe handicap except on the poster or a telethon.

Perspective

The presence of students with severe handicaps provides valuable social, emotional, and personal perspectives that cannot be realized in their absence. We suspect that a mild case of acne is not so devastating when there is a student in the next room with no arms and no legs. A bikini-inhibiting appendectomy scar is less worthy of concern when the girl down the hall has spina bifida. And depression is not so severe after missing an "A" by one point when you ride to school with a friend who experiences total deafness, total blindness, and severe retardation.

Certainly, we are not advocating a caste system of "haves" and "have nots," nor a condescending "lucky me-poor you" mentality. On the contrary, only through individually meaningful, comprehensive, and longitudinal exposure and experience can we realize how important it is to learn to live, work, and play together and affirm and enjoy the beauties and inherent value of individual differences.

Finally, we now know that there are many nonhandicapped persons who realize a tremendous range of emotional and social benefits from their involvements with persons who experience severe handicaps, including realistically enhanced self-concepts, the important maturational feelings that emanate from learning to assume responsibility, the expansive enlightenment that comes best, if not only, from sincere attempts to communicate with, understand, and like those who are a little different than usual or who are not members of our overly restrictive "in group" (Voeltz, 1980, 1982).

BENEFITS TO SEVERELY HANDICAPPED STUDENTS

It is the unduly protective assumption of many that segregated schools are in the best interest of students with severe handicaps. Comments such as the following are heard from this group: "If they are segregated, they will not be subjected to ridicule and exploitation by nonhandicapped students who do not know better." "No one should be reminded every day of his/her handicapping condition." "Functioning in the presence of nonhandicapped students can only serve to exaggerate difficulties, and ultimately this will have the effect of lowering his/her self-concept." Such assumptions do not sufficiently address the reality that many interactions between nonhandicapped students and students with severe handicaps occur after school, on weekends, during vacation, etc., in churches, stores, neighborhoods, and many other community environments in spite of the possibility of ridicule and exploitation or a "lowered self-concept." Thus, just as the public school experience should prepare the nonhandicapped to function meaningfully with students who experience severe handicaps, so should it prepare students with severe handicaps to function with nonhandicapped students and other nonhandicapped persons.

A severely handicapped student based in a special education classroom in a chronologically-age-appropriate, regular, neighborhood school has opportunities to realize benefits from many kinds of interactions with nonhandicapped students that would not be available if the same student were based in a segregated school. Nonhandicapped students exhibit both a higher frequency and often a more diverse and higher quality of social behaviors than do some of their peers who experience severe handicaps. Indeed, comparisons of integrated and segregated free play settings have demonstrated that in integrated settings nonhandicapped peers initiate social behavior up to five times more often than handicapped peers in segregated settings (Hecimovic, Fox, Shores, & Strain, in press). Also the social responses of students with handicaps elicit a significantly higher proportion of positive return responses from nonhandicapped peers in integrated settings than from other handicapped children in segregated settings (Fox, Gunter, Brady, Bambara, McGill, & Shores, 1984). Thus as compared to segregated settings, in integrated settings students with severe handicaps are provided the opportunity to be exposed to and reciprocate to a broader range of social interaction behaviors as well as have their social behaviors reacted to. Some of these beneficial interactions can be characterized as of four nonmutually exclusive types; proximal, helping, service, and reciprocal.

Proximal Interactions

Proximal interactions are those in which some type of sensory contact is made between a student with severe handicaps and a nonhandicapped person, and as such provide the foundation upon which most other types of interactions are based. Examples of proximal interactions that occur regularly are students with severe handicaps using an adjacent locker, using the same bathroom, and sitting in a wheelchair at the same table with nonhandicapped students during lunch. Some of the benefits to students with severe handicaps include learning how to function in ever changing environments with wide variations in noise levels, movements, objects, and color schemes; and becoming more aware of popular chronologically-age-appropriate fashions, music, language, and gestures.

Helping Interactions

Helping interactions are those in which a nonhandicapped student voluntarily provides direct assistance or instruction to a student with a severe handicapping condition(s). If nonhandicapped students are in the sensory presence of students with severe handicaps, a reasonable number will become interested in learning how and how not to help. Learning to push a wheelchair to and from the playground, to teach the use of a vending machine in the school cafeteria, to become a buddy during music, art, or an extracurricular activity, and to convert dead time to constructive play time are but a few examples. Some of the benefits students with severe handicaps can realize are learning to perform skills across persons, places, materials, and language cues; learning the conditions under which one should accept assistance and when to indicate appropriately a desire to function independently; and establishing social and affective relationships that can become more reciprocal in nature.

Service Interactions

Service interactions are those in which a nonhandicapped person, as a function of employment responsibilities, provides a service to a student with severe handicaps. In such interactions two skill clusters are critical: nonhandicapped persons must know how to provide services to the student, and the student must know how to use the services of nonhandicapped persons. Some of the situations in which a student with a severe handicap can learn to use such services include responding appropriately to crossing guards, communicating nonverbally to school and community bus drivers and school medical personnel, and indicating food preferences to cafeteria personnel.

Reciprocal Interactions

In the reciprocal interaction, nonhandicapped students and students with severe handicaps are not merely occupying the same physical space; a nonhandicapped student is not volunteering to help nor getting paid to provide a service. Rather, the two are relating to each other and both are accruing personal benefits from the relationship. Playing a game during a free period, participating in an after school sporting event, and attending a school party are but a few examples. Although relatively difficult to generate, particularly as chronological age increases, reciprocal interactions are important for students with severe handicaps because they are likely to be maintained for significant time periods, because they engender increased understanding between persons, because they help students learn to occupy their leisure time in more constructive and enjoyable ways, and because others viewing the mutual fulfillment may desire similar interactions.

THE REGULAR CLASSROOM TEACHER'S ROLE

Regular class teachers have a definite role to play in assisting students with severe handicaps to become integral members of the student body in regular schools. One basic ingredient in the regular class teacher's role is the need to work cooperatively with special class teachers in preparing the environment to promote optimal integration conditions. This cooperative teacher relationship has been found to be a key factor in the successful integration of students with severe handicaps into regular school programs and activities (Hamre-Nietupski, 1980).

Once a cooperative relationship between regular and special educators has been established, the role of the regular class teacher in integration efforts can begin to mature. First, regular class teachers can provide their nonhandicapped students with opportunities to interact with students who experience severe handicaps. While logically it may not be appropriate for nonhandicapped students and students with severe handicaps to compete in certain academic and highly competitive tasks, regular class teachers can work cooperatively with special class teachers to provide integrated school experiences for students with severe handicaps. For example, at the elementary school level, regular class teachers can help facilitate integration by accepting students with severe handicaps into their classrooms during selected activities such as homeroom, art, music, recess, holiday celebrations, birthday parties, show-and-tell times, and/or rest periods. There are other ways regular class teachers can help facilitate integration. For instance, they can encourage their nonhandicapped students to visit the special education classroom(s) to work as tutors, or simply to spend a little time with a friend who experiences a severe handicap. In addition, regular class teachers can join with special class teachers in providing opportunities for interaction between nonhandicapped students and students with severe handicaps in the school cafeteria, on the playground, at assembly programs, in the hallways and at the bus loading and unloading zones.

Regular class teachers at the high school level can also provide opportunities for interaction between students with severe handicaps and nonhandicapped students. For example, at the high school level, students might interact during lunch, in some vocational training related activities, and during special events such as holiday parties. In addition, many high school students have successfully served as tutors in special classes for students with severe handicaps.

A crucial role for regular class teachers involves the enhancement of interactions between nonhandicapped students and students with severe handicaps in integrated situations, when interactions do not spontaneously occur. Regular class teachers can implement, with special class teachers, organizational arrangements and procedures to facilitate interactions in integrated situations. Research has indicated that providing interaction opportunities is not always enough, since interactions between nonhandicapped students and students with severe handicaps do not always spontaneously occur when opportunities are provided (Guralnick, 1980). Thus, teachers may be called upon to promote interactions. Interactions between nonhandicapped students and students with severe handicaps can be promoted much as interactions between other groups of students are promoted in any classroom made up of students with a variety of intellectual, racial, social, and economic characteristics. Teachers can foster interactions, for example, by organizing small groups to work on cooperative goals (Rynders, Johnson, Johnson, & Schmidt, 1980) and/or by encouraging and reinforcing interactions among nonhandicapped students and students with severe handicaps (Stainback, Stainback, Raschke, & Anderson, 1981).

The final role of the regular class teacher, to be discussed here, is to teach nonhandicapped students about severely handicapped students in order to promote interactions among these students. Methods and materials have been developed that regular class teachers can use in such training (see Section III and Chapter 13). Many of the most recent methods go beyond (or replace) the teaching of nonhandicapped students about handicapping conditions (e.g., categories of handicapping conditions, genetic defects, and chromosomal abnormalities). These methods focus on teaching nonhandicapped students respect for individual differences and the benefits that can be derived from interactions with persons of different abilities and backgrounds. Thus, one of the regular class teacher's roles might be to serve as a trainer of nonhandicapped students in regard to human differences as well as appropriate reactions to human differences that could help foster positive interactions between nonhandicapped students and students who experience severe handicaps.

In summary, regular class teachers can (a) provide nonhandicapped students with opportunities to interact with students who experience severe handicaps (b) encourage and reinforce interactions between the two groups, and (c) train nonhandicapped students in regard to human differences.

THE ROLE OF THE SPECIAL CLASS TEACHER

The special class teacher functions as an advocate and program planner for handicapped students in regular schools. As such, she or he plays a pivotal role in the integration process. It is the responsibility of the special class teacher to see that integrated learning experiences are included in the educational programs of students with severe handicaps. Through the work of the special class teacher, ongoing daily integration of handicapped students into normalized educational environments can be established and maintained. In relation to fulfilling this roll the special class teacher has several duties.

An initial as well as ongoing duty of the special teacher in regard to integration efforts is the dissemination of information. Information concerning the value of integration to all students should be provided both regular school personnel and community members. Similarly, it is the special class teacher who serves as the access person for integration information available in the literature about how to facilitate integration and positive interactions between students with severe handicaps and nonhandicapped students.

Usually, it is also the job of the special class teacher to initiate and organize integration activities. While integration activities should be arranged as shared efforts between regular and special school personnel, it is often the responsibility of the special class teacher to initiate such activities. To promote maintenance and reduce disruption during the school day, special class teachers, in conjunction with regular school personnel, can schedule integration activities as ongoing experiences within naturally occurring daily school activities.

Another duty of the special class teacher in regard to integration efforts is to provide direct training of appropriate social behaviors to students with severe handicaps (Gaylord-Ross, Haring, Breen, & Pitts-Conway, 1984). While promoting integration/interaction experiences with nonhandicapped students, teachers should provide systematic training to enhance the social skill development of severely handicapped students who lack appropriate social skills. Special attention should be focused on promoting the development of those skills that will facilitate the integration of students into natural school and community activities and settings. Information about how to assess and train the social skills of handicapped students can be found in chapters 9 and 10 and Gaylord-Ross, et al, 1984.

Finally, it is the special class teacher, along with other school personnel, who will need to monitor and evaluate the integration experiences of students with severe handicaps. The special class teacher will need to engage in ongoing evaluation of both the quantity and quality of integration experiences occurring throughout the school day. Inherent in evaluation is the maintenance of records and modifications of those integration activities that do not result in positive experiences for both students with severe handicaps and nonhandicapped students.

In summary, special class teachers can facilitate integration by (a) disseminating information on integration to regular school personnel and community members, (b) initiating and organizing integration activities, (c) training students with severe handicaps to display appropriate social behaviors and (d) monitoring and evaluating integration experiences between nonhandicapped students and students with severe handicaps.

CONCLUSION

The success of integration efforts between nonhandicapped students and students with severe handicaps is important since both nonhandicapped students and students with severe handicaps can benefit from well-planned and organized integration experiences. In integrated school environments, nonhandicapped students are provided unique opportunities to learn firsthand about human differences and similarities and how to approach and interact with members of society who experience severe handicaps. Researchers have found that,

generally speaking, nonhandicapped students who have had opportunities to interact with severely handicapped students hold more positive and accepting attitudes toward them than nonhandicapped students
who have not had such opportunities (e.g., Voeltz, 1980; Voeltz, 1982).
Such interactions can also reduce nonhandicapped students' fear of students with severe handicaps and promote understanding and acceptance
(McHale & Simeonsson, 1980). Thus, nonhandicapped students can
profit from interactions with students who experience severe handicaps.

Students with severe handicaps can also profit from interactions with
nonhandicapped students. In integrated school situations, students
with severe handicaps are given opportunities for more expanded
and normalized learning experiences. Egel, Richman, and Koegel
(1981) found that students with severe handicaps can profit in regard
to learning basic educational tasks from observing nonhandicapped
student peer models. Guralnick (in press) found that students with
severe handicaps displayed fewer inappropriate play behaviors while in
integrated as opposed to segregated situations. In addition, researchers
have found that more social initiations are displayed toward students
with severe handicaps in integrated settings than segregated settings
(Hecimovic et al., in press; Fox et al., 1984), and as a result, students
with severe handicaps themselves often display more social responses
in integrated settings than segregated settings. Finally, Strain (1983)
found that students labeled autistic generalized newly acquired social
behaviors considerably better in an integrated setting than a segregated
one. Strain found clear benefits to integration and concluded that "it is
quite reasonable to question the predominant and pervasive segregation
of autistic-like children into 'handicapped-only' groups" (p. 34). Thus,
educational benefits for all students involved can be realized when both
regular and special teachers work together to foster positive integration.

Finally, before closing this chapter, it should be noted that all of us,
including the authors, tend to look for evidence, particularly "scientific"
evidence, that integration produces clear and measurable social or
other gains for students with severe handicaps and/or nonhandicapped
students. However, while the possible benefits of integration are
important, the decision to integrate should not be based purely on
the research evidence regarding the possible benefits. Instead, we
should recognize that whether or not to integrate is a moral issue, not a
"scientific" issue regarding benefits. Experimentation and research can
be of help in assisting us to find the best ways or methods to achieve
integration as well as any possible benefits, but whether we should or
should not integrate is a moral or *value* issue. As noted by Biklen (in
press):

> Science cannot offer a yes or no decision on integration. An analogy
> may make the point clearer. At the time of the American Civil War,
> should Abraham Lincoln have asked to see the scientific evidence on

the benefits of ending slavery? Should he have consulted with "the experts," perhaps a sociologist, and economist, a political scientist? Of course not. Slavery is not now and was not than an issue for science. It is a moral issue. But, just for a moment, suppose that an economist had been able to demonstrate that Blacks would suffer economically, as would the entire South, from emancipation. Would that justify keeping slavery? And suppose a political scientist had argued that Blacks had no experience with democracy, they were not ready for it. Would that have justified extending slavery? Or imagine that a sociologist could have advised Lincoln against abolishing slavery on the grounds that it would destroy the basic social structure of Southern plantations, towns, and cities. From a racist perspective, all of the arguments might have seemed "true." But could they really justify slavery? Of course not. Slavery has no justification. (p. 16-17)

Let us draw another analogy. Suppose that researchers found that the vast majority of students tend to be nonaccepting or rejecting of students from very low socioeconomic backgrounds, particularly those with poor interaction skills. They would rather not have them in "their" schools. Suppose it was even found that many students ridiculed students from low socioeconomic backgrounds and made fun of the them. Or, suppose that researchers found that most students and teachers rejected selected students considered by them to be "ugly." Should we segregate students with low socioeconomic backgrounds who do not have good social interaction skills or students considered by others to be ugly? Based on the current values of society at large, we would not likely consider segregating them. The point is that if researchers or teachers should in the future find that students with severe handicaps are rejected by their nonhandicapped peers, it does not necessarily follow that they should be segregated. Whether they should be segregated is a value judgment. Rather than segregate, we might make the value judgment to try harder to find ways to help all students to respect each other and to show kindness to each other.

As can be gleaned from the above analogies, whether or not to integrate students with severe handicaps into regular schools is a moral, not a research, issue. The authors have made a value judgment that integrated education for all students is the best and most humane way to proceed. In the remainder of this book we attempt to offer some suggestions about how to make integration of students with severe handicaps into regular schools a rewarding experience for all students.

REFERENCES

Biklen, D. (in press) *The complete school: Integrating special and regular education.* Columbia University: Teachers College Press.

Brady, M. & Dennis, H. (1984). Integrating severely handicapped learners: Potential teacher liability in community based programs. *Remedial and Special Education*, 5, 29-36.

Brown, L., Branston, M., Hamre-Neitupski, S., Johnson, F., Wilcox, B.,

& Gruenewald, L. (1979).   A rationale for comprehensive longitudinal interactions between severely handicapped students and non-handicapped students and other citizens. *AAESPH Review*, *4*, 3-14.

Brown, L., Ford, A., Nisbet, J., Sweet, M., Donnellan, A., & Gruenewald, L. (1983).   Opportunities available when severely handicapped students attend chronological age appropriate regular schools. *The Journal of The Association for the Severely Handicapped, 8*, 16-24.

Egel, A., Richman, G., & Koegel, R. (1981) Normal peer models and autistic children learning. *Journal of Applied Behavior Analysis, 14*, 3-11.

Fox, J., Gunter, P., Brady, M., Bambara, L., McGill, P., & Shores, R. (1984). *Using multiple peer exemplars to develop generalized social responding of an autistic girl.* Manuscript submitted for publication.

Gaylord-Ross, R., Haring, T., Breen, C. , & Pitts-Conway, U. (1984). The training and generalization of social interaction skills with autistic youth. *Journal of Applied Behavior Analysis, 17*, 229-247.

Guralnick, M. J. (in press).   The social behavior of preschool children at different developmental levels: Effects of group composition. *Journal of Experimental Child Psychology* .

Guralnick, M. J. (1980).   Social interactions among preschool children. *Exceptional Children, 46*, 248-253.

Hamre-Nietupski, S. (1980). *Sensitizing non-handicapped persons to severely handicapped students in regular public school settings.* Paper presented at the National Conference of The Association for the Severely Handicapped, Los Angeles (1981).

Hamre-Nietupski, S., & Nietupski, J. (1981).   Integral involvement of severely handicapped students within regular public schools. *Journal of the Association for the Severely Handicapped, 6*, 30-39.

Hecimovic, A., Fox, J., Shores, R., & Strain, P. (in press). The effects of integrated and segregated settings on the generalization of newly-acquired social behaviors of socially withdrawn preschoolers. *Behavioral Assessment.*

McHale, S., & Simeonsson, R. (1980).   Effects of interaction on non-handicapped children's attitudes toward autistic children. *American Journal of Mental Deficiency, 85*, 18-24.

Nirje, B. (1969).   The normalization principle and its human management implications. In R. Kugel, & W. Wolfenberger (Eds.) *Changing patterns in residential services for the mentally retarded* (pp. 179-195). Washington: President's Committee on Mental Retardation.

Pennsylvania association for retarded children v. Commonwealth of Pennsylvania, 343, F. Supp., 279 (E.D. Pa. 1972).

Reynolds, M., & Birch, J. (1977). *Teaching exceptional children all in America's schools.* Reston: The Council for Exceptional Children (1980).

Rynders, J., Johnson, R., Johnson, D., & Schmidt, B. (1980).   Producing positive interaction among Down Syndrome and non-handicapped teenagers through cooperative goal structuring.   *American Journal of Mental Deficiency, 85*, 268-273.

Stainback, S., & Stainback, W. (1980).   *Educating children with severe maladaptive behaviors.* New York: Grune and Stratton.

Stainback, S., & Stainback, W. (1981). A review of research on interactions between severely handicapped and non-handicapped students. *The Journal of the Association for the Severely Handicapped, 6*, 23-29.

Stainback, W., Stainback, S. Raschke, D., & Anderson, R. (1981). Three methods for encouraging interactions between severely retarded and non-handicapped students. *Education and Training of the Mentally Retarded, 16,* 188-192.

Strain, P. (1983). Generalization of autistic children's social behavior change: Effects of developmentally integrated and segregated settings. *Analysis and Intervention in Developmental Disabilities, 3,* 23-34.

Voeltz, L. (1980). Children's attitudes toward handicapped peers. *American Journal of Mental Deficiency, 84,* 455-464.

Voeltz, L. Effects of structured interactions with severely handicapped peers on children's attitudes, *American Journal of Mental Deficiency, 1982, 86,* 380-390.

Section II

Interactions in Integrated Settings

Chapter 3

Providing Opportunities for Interaction

As noted in chapter 2, the trend to providing programming in regular public school for students with handicaps is gaining widespread support. One of the benefits of integrating students with severe handicaps and nonhandicaped students is the possibility for increased interaction between the two groups. Researchers have found that interaction can benefit both students with severe handicaps and nonhandicapped students (Schutz, Williams, Iverson, & Duncan, 1984; Stainback & Stainback, 1981).

Thus, it is important for teachers to arrange the environment so that opportunities are actually available for interaction between students experiencing severe handicaps and nonhandicapped students. In this chapter, several ways of providing opportunities for interaction are discussed. The methods discussed are meant only to serve as examples. There are numerous possibilities for providing opportunities for interaction and teachers should use whatever ways are available to them. Also, it should be stressed that opportunities for interaction should not be episodic in nature. Natural, ongoing opportunities for interaction should be a normal part of every school day.

OPPORTUNITIES FOR INTERACTION

Opportunities for interaction can be provided in many ways. Outlined here are several practical and easy-to-implement methods.

1. One way to foster interaction opportunities is for the school principal and regular and special class teachers to work together to schedule handicapped and nonhandicapped students during the same period in the school cafeteria, at the bus loading and unloading zones, on the playground, in school assembly

programs, and/or in whatever "regular" classes possible. Obviously, when students with severe handicaps and nonhandicapped students are scheduled to be in the same place at the same time, the opportunities for interaction are enhanced.

2. Special and regular class teachers can join their classes together for special events such as Halloween, Thanksgiving, birthday, and Christmas parties. It may also be possible for special and regular class teachers to join their classes for selected recreational, art, music, and other activities. In addition, school-wide joint work projects can be organized to provide students with severe handicaps and nonhandicapped students other interaction opportunities. Projects such as school beautification or litter clean-up campaigns can be jointly sponsored and carried out by students with severe handicaps and nonhandicapped students. Activities requiring a diversified range of skills are optimal for joint work projects so that each student can contribute to the project according to his or her individual abilities.

3. Tutoring and buddy systems can be organized to provide additional interaction opportunities (Kohl, Moses, Stettner-Eaton, 1984; McHale, Olley, Marcus, & Simeonsson, 1981). Nonhandicapped students can serve as tutors for students with severe handicaps. This tutoring can occur in either the special or regular classroom. Also, buddy systems can be organized wherein nonhandicapped students and students with severe handicaps are paired together as companions during fire drills or field trips. It is critical that such interactions be organized to foster mutual respect between students.

4. Opportunities can be arranged through "special" friends projects. Teachers can simply arrange for nonhandicapped students and students with severe handicaps to spend time together in social and leisure activities of interest to both students. The emphasis is on the development of normalized friendships and social interaction between the students. Teacher intrusion is kept to a minimum and nonhandicapped students are *not* encouraged to "tutor" or "teach" their handicapped peer(s).

It should be possible, with planning and cooperation among school personnel, for students with severe handicaps to have the opportunity to interact with nonhandicapped students for at least part of each school day. As noted in Chapter 2, while it might not be beneficial to some students with severe handicaps for them to be placed in certain academic and highly competitive tasks with nonhandicapped students, it is still possible to provide opportunites for interaction between the two groups of students. The opportunities provided should be a part of regularly scheduled school activities as much as possible. In no instance should special, planned opportunites for interaction be used as substitutes for daily natural and on-going interaction opportunities.

In the remainder of this chapter, two specific ways of providing opportunities for interaction are discussed in more depth. The purpose in discussing them is to point out several crucial factors that should be considered when providing opportunities for interaction.

Cooperative Work Projects

There are projects that need to be accomplished in any school that both students with severe handicaps and nonhandicapped students can work together to complete. The projects should be set up so that all students involved can contribute to their successful completion. Examples of some possible projects include decorating a school wall or bulletin board, planting flowers or shrubs on the school grounds, rearranging the cafeteria for an assembly, or making props for a school play.

An example of how a cooperative work project could be implemented follows. A regular and special classroom teacher might coordinate times at which their students could work together on designated projects. Following this the students with handicaps and the nonhandicapped students would be jointly responsible for actually planning and carrying out the projects(s) under the guidance of their teachers. One such task might involve the planting and maintenance of a flower garden on school grounds. Discussions involving the students and teachers would have to take place to determine where the garden should be planted, what flowers should be included, and how to arrange the students' time schedules to give them opportunites to work on the project. After the planning stage, the garden project could get under way. From one such project other joint projects and activities could be planned.

It should be noted that the students with severe handicaps and the nonhandicapped students should be approximately the same chronological age and should work on age-appropriate activities. While many professionals in the past have felt that it was not possible, due to mental age functioning, for students with severe handicaps to work on age-appropriate activities, this belief is changing (Brown, Branston, Hamre-Nietupski, Pumpian, et al., 1979.) Students with severe handicaps can make meaningful contributions to numerous age-appropriate projects or activities. A few examples have already been cited. Also, the projects selected should be real and functional. It would be a mistake to have the students work on a "made-up" project, one that has no real meaning or purpose. We have found that most students' enthusiasm wanes quickly when they are faced with nonfunctional, meaningless tasks. In short, any project selected should be age-appropriate, worthwhile, and challenging to both the nonhandicapped students and the students with severe handicaps.

Joint Play Sessions

Joint play sessions can also be used to enhance positive interaction behaviors between students with severe handicaps and nonhandicapped students. This method involves an organized play situation in which the regular and special teachers cooperatively plan group games and activities that both of their classes can participate in jointly during at least some of their recess periods. The games selected should be positive, high probability activities that are age appropriate for the students. The games should also be arranged so that successful participation can be expected from both the students with severe handicaps and the nonhandicapped students.

Unique and enjoyable but fairly simple games are particularly useful. The games chosen, although not unnecessarily complicated, should present a challenge to both the students with severe handicaps and the nonhandicapped students. Often those involving the influences of the physical environment are fun, challenging, and a good learning experience. One set of games that meet these criteria for most children are parachute activities. One way to play a parachute game is to place a ball in the center and have the children grasp the edge of the parachute. The object of the game is for the children to knock the ball off by lifting their arms and hands and getting air under the parachute. While this game can be played without an excess of rules and complicated movements, it is an enjoyable, novel experience for most children and presents a challenge to them. It should be noted that for children who have poor grasp or arm movement in either of the classes, this particular activity may not be applicable or may require modification. The physical as well as other abilities of the children involved should influence game selection.

A word of optimism about what students with severe handicaps can do should be inserted here. Unfortunately, we sometimes determine that a game (activity or project) is too complex for some students, especially students experiencing severe handicaps, when it is *not* too complex or difficult. The real problem is our own inability to adapt the activity and/or physical/social environment so the student(s) can participate (at least partially), and/or to provide the students with the kind of assistance necessary for them to participate. Baumgart et al., (1982) have pointed out that students with severe handicaps have been excluded unnecessarily or excused from numerous activities because they could not perform "adequately." They also outlined ways in which students with severe handicaps can participate or partially participate in activities we may consider too complex or difficult for them.

Finally, to carry out joint play successfully, it may be necessary to train some handicapped students in appropriate play behavior. This training may also be needed for some members of the nonhandicapped class. Both decreasing inappropriate play behavior—such as refusal to play, lack of sustained play, and throwing toys or objects—as well as the building of appropriate behaviors, such as learning to play cooperatively and sharing, may need to be included in play training sequences. Fortunately, there has been a great deal of research and ideas published about how to decrease inappropriate and teach appropriate play and social skills (e.g., Hill, Wehman, & Horst, 1982; Wehman, 1977; 1979; Wehman & Marchant, 1978). Such training sequences may considerably influence the potential success of the joint play approach to interactions.

CONCLUSION

Opportunities for students with severe handicaps and nonhandicapped students to interact can occur as part of typical school activities. In most instances, students can be provided opportunities to interact in normally scheduled school activities such as recess, lunch, assembly programs, art, music, special school projects, and field trips. In other words, opportunties for interaction can and should become an integral part of ongoing school programs and activities (Donder & York, 1984).

While integrated school experiences can be provided for all students with severe handicaps across a variety of school settings, it should be stressed here that *the specific form or exact nature of the integrated experiences should be individualized according to the age, needs, and capabilities of the student(s) involved.* In addition to the age and characteristics of the students involved, the specific methods used will depend on factors such as the cooperative spirit of the special and regular class teachers and the organizational structure of the school. Fortunately, there are many creative and talented teachers who are continually coming up with excellent ideas about how students with severe handicaps can become integrated members of the general public school population.

It should be noted that integrating students with severe handicaps, on an individual basis, into selected regular school programs is not as difficult as it might at first glance appear to be. When integration occurs, there are generally only a very small number of students with severe handicaps involved. Even if an entire class of students with severe handicaps were to be included in a regular class activity the number of students involved would be small. (Only four or five students are typically enrolled in a class for students with severe handicaps.) In addition, in schools in which students with severe handicaps are provided educational services, special class teachers and aides are usually available to provide support and assistance for integrated programming.

The methods outlined in this chapter are meant only to serve as examples of how interaction can occur between students with severe handicaps and nonhandicapped students. There are numerous other ways interactions can occur. Opportunities for interactions should be available in the hallways, restrooms, when riding the bus, and in many classroom activities such as show-and-tell times and rest times. The number of possible ways is almost endless. Also, opportunities for interactions between handicapped and nonhandicapped students can be provided at all levels of schooling. As noted earlier, at the high school level, students with handicaps and nonhandicapped students might interact during lunch, in some vocational training related activities, and in certain science projects such as collecting various types of leaves from trees to be analyzed.

In summary, in addition to physically locating students with severe handicaps in regular schools, every effort should be made to integrate students with severe handicaps into as many regular school activities *as possible*. In other words, students with severe handicaps should *not* spend the entire school day in the special class environment. There are many regular school activities (or environments) that students with severe handicaps can participate in or at least partially participate in.

REFERENCES

Baumgart, D., Brown, L., Pumpian, I., Nisbet, J., Ford, A., Sweet, M., Messina, R., & Schroeder, J. (1982). Principle of partial participation and individualized adaptations in educational programs for severely handicapped students. *The Journal of the Association for the Severely Handicapped, 7*, 17-27.

Brown, L., Branston, M., Hamre-Nietupski, S., Pumpian, I., Certo, N., & Gruenewald, L. (1979). A strategy for developing chronological age appropriate and functional curricular content for severely handicapped adolescents and young adults. *Journal of Special Education, 13*, 81-90.

Donder, D., & York, R. (1984). Integration of students with severe handicaps. In N. Certo, N. Haring, & R. York (Eds.) *Public school integration of severely handicapped students.* (pp. 1-14). Baltimore: Paul Brookes.

Hill, J., Wehman, P., & Horst, G. (1982). Toward generalization of appropriate leisure and social behavior in severely handicapped youth: Pinball Machine Use. *The Journal of the Association for the Severely Handicapped, 6*, 1982.

Kohl, F., Moses, L., & Stettner-Eaton, B. (1984). A systematic training program for teaching non-handicapped students to be instructional trainers for severely handicapped schoolmates. In N. Certo, N. Haring, E. R. York (Eds.) *Public school integration of severely handicapped students.* (pp. 185-196). Baltimore: Paul Brookes.

McHale, S., Olley, J., Marcus, L., & Simeonsson, R. (1981). Non-handicapped peers as tutors for autistic children. *Exceptional Children, 48*, 263-265.

Schutz, R., Williams, W., Iverson, G., & Duncan, D. (1984). Social integration of severely handicapped students. In N. Certo, N. Haring, & R. York (Eds.) *Public school integration of severely handicapped students.* (pp. 15-42). Baltimore: Paul Brookes.

Stainback, W., & Stainback, S. (1981). A review of research on interactions between severely handicapped and non-handicapped students. *The Journal of the Association for the Severely Handicapped, 6*, 23-29.

Wehman, P. (1977). *Helping the mentally retarded acquire play skills: A behavioral approach.* Springfield, IL: Charles C Thomas.

Wehman, P. (1979). Instructional strategies for improving toy play skills of severely handicapped children. *AAESPH Review, 4*, 125-135.

Wehman, P., & Marchant, J. (1978). Improving free play skills of severely retarded children. *American Journal of Occupational Therapy, 32*, 100-104.

Chapter 4

Assessing Opportunities for Interaction

This chapter describes a checklist formulated to help estimate the degree to which students with severe handicaps placed in regular schools are integrated into various regular school environments. Purposes for which school personnel might want to use the checklist, as well as suggested ways of improving a school's score, are also discussed.

DEVELOPMENT AND INTERPRETATION

The 14 items included in the checklist were determined by analyzing and listing the various environments within a regular school setting in which students with severe handicaps and nonhandicapped students have been known to participate. Several principals and regular and special class teachers reviewed the list and suggested modifications. Each of the 14 items explores a selected environment such as the playground, lunchroom, hallways, and certain regular class activities (See Figure 1).

The checklist may be used in any elementary or secondary regular school setting in which students with severe handicaps receive educational services. Administration of the instrument requires less than 10 minutes. An individual who is intimately familiar with the activities of handicapped students in the school, such as the special teacher or the principal, should provide the data. The accuracy of the information obtained will be directly related to the level of knowledge of that individual.

Response options to each statement included in the checklist are on a 5-point Likert-type scale. These options are designed to reflect various degrees of integration based on the approximate percentage of students with severe handicaps integrated in a designated school environment. The options range from *all* (i.e., 100% of the students experiencing severe handicaps in the school are integrated in the environment) to *none*, in which 0% are integrated. Each of the possible options

FIGURE 1
Severely Handicapped Integration Checklist

Date _____ Name of School _____

Name and Position of Person Providing Information _____

Directions: After reading each question, put an X under the category that best reflects how many students with severe handicaps engage in the specified activity or environment.

Do students with severe handicaps:	All (100%)	Most (>50% but <100%)	Some (Approx. 50%)	Few (<50% but >0%)	None (0%)
1. Ride the same school buses that nonhandicapped students ride?					
2. Have their classrooms located throughout a regular school building with classrooms for the nonhandicapped?					
3. Attend school assembly programs with nonhandicapped students?					
4. Eat lunch in the school cafeteria during the same time as nonhandicapped students?					
5. Eat lunch at the same tables in the school cafeteria with nonhandicapped students?					

6. Share recess (or recreational times) with nonhandicapped students?					
7. Go on school field trips with nonhandicapped students?					
8. Share special events such as Halloween and Thanksgiving parties or football homecoming celebrations with nonhandicapped children?					
9. Share homeroom with nonhandicapped students?					
10. Use the same bathroom as nonhandicapped students?					
11. Use the school hallways at the same time as nonhandicapped students?					
12. Share one or more classes such as art, music, and/or PE with nonhandicapped students?					
13. Have their school pictures interspersed with their nonhandicapped peers throughout school publications (e.g., yearbook, newsletters, or displays)?					
14. Share school jobs and responsibilities with nonhandicapped students (e.g., arranging chairs in the gym for an upcoming assembly program)?					

Scoring procedures: Determine the score for each question (None = 0; Few = 1; Some = 2; Most = 3; All = 4.) Add the individual scores to obtain the total score.   TOTAL SCORE _____ receives a point score which is totaled to arrive at a score for a school's integration rating on the overall checklist.

The score for each item is a 4 if *all* (100%) is marked; 3 if *most* (>50% but <100%) is marked; 2 if *some* (=50%) is marked; 1 if *few* (<50% but >0%) is marked; and 0 if *none* (0%) is marked. Possible total scores range from 0 to 56. Although a score of 56 indicates the highest level of integration, the determination of the most appropriate score for any particular school should reflect the needs of the students in that school. Generally speaking, however, the higher the score the better the situation in regard to the integration of students with severe handicaps within the regular school.

USES

The Severely Handicapped Integration Checklist (SHIC) may be used by a variety of individuals to obtain an objective measure of the "integratedness" of a school in regard to students with severe handicaps located in the building. The teacher of a class for handicapped students, for example, could use the checklist to evaluate the degree to which integrated activities are provided for his or her students. Results can yield a clear picture or relatively strong and weak areas of integration, providing guidance for the teacher in subsequent efforts to upgrade the level of integration.

Similarly, the instrument may be useful to other educators. A principal could use the checklist to evaluate an entire school. Consultants for school districts could use it in a systematic evaluation of the schools under their supervision to assist in guiding integration suggestions. State department personnel could use the SHIC to determine state progress in integration activities. The instrument may also be helpful to outside evaluators and researchers as a tool for obtaining an objective measure of the degree of integration within a school. The relative ease, speed, objectivity, and simplicity of scoring the instrument make the SHIC a practical, viable means of collecting useful data.

HOW TO CORRECT LOW SCORES

If a school scores low on the Severely Handicapped Integration Checklist, several steps should be taken. First, determine the environment(s) in which students with severe handicaps are not integrated. Second, determine why integration is not occurring in these environments. Third, find a solution or way of correcting the situation.

If, for example, students with severe handicaps are not integrated on school buses because nonhandicapped students might ridicule them or treat them in an unaccepting or cruel manner, then school personnel might attempt to change the attitudes and behaviors of the nonhandicapped students.

If students with severe handicaps are not integrated into a particular class (e.g., art, music, or physical education) because they are so profoundly handicapped that they could not profit from the instruction, then school personnel might determine alternative environments or situations where integration is feasible. Small groups of nonhandicapped students from a physical education class, for instance, might visit the special class periodically to tutor students experiencing profound handicaps in rudimentary PE activities such as gaining motor control of head movements. The nonhandicapped students might, in the process, learn something about physiology, gain a better understanding of persons experiencing profound handicaps, and possibly develop new friendships. At the same time, the students with profound handicaps might improve their motor skills as well as profit from the social stimulation, as a result of the additional individual attention they receive.

CONCLUSION

Integrated school experiences can be provided for all students with severe handicaps across a variety of school settings. However, as noted in the previous chapter, the specific form or exact nature of the integrated experiences should be individualized according to the age, needs, and capabilities of the student(s) involved. With planning and cooperation among school personnel, it should be possible for nonhandicapped students and students with severe handicaps to have the opportunity to interact for at least a part of each school day. It should be stressed that whenever possible, teachers and administrators should provide interaction opportunities as a natural part of each school day as opposed to planning special, episodic opportunities for interactions.

Integrating students with severe handicaps in selected regular school environments may be only the first step. It may be necessary to train both nonhandicapped students and students with severe handicaps in appropriate and positive ways of interacting with each other. Ways of promoting positive interactions between students with severe handicaps and nonhandicapped students are discussed in the next chapter.

Chapter 5

Promoting Interactions

In Chapter 3, the authors outlined some practical ways of integrating students experiencing handicaps with nonhandicapped students in many regular school activities and programs. However, it is increasingly being recognized that the mere integration of handicapped with nonhandicapped students does not always lead to positive interactions. Researchers have found that interactions do not always occur spontaneously between students in these groups (Faught, Balleweg, Crow, Van Den Pol, 1983; Guralnick, 1980). In other words, interactions between students with severe handicaps and nonhandicapped students do not always occur as a result of *integration alone*. In addition to physically integrating students with severe handicaps into various public school environments, specialized programming may have to occur if the positive interactions are to take place. In other words, the critical component may not be the simple presence of nonhandicapped students and students with severe handicaps in the same school or class, but the way in which interactions among these students are systematically guided and encouraged.

The purpose of this chapter is to delineate three methods teachers could use to promote positive interactions between students with severe handicaps and nonhandicapped students. These are (a) classroom organization, structure, and materials; (b) training students with severe handicaps in interactional skills; and (c) training nonhandicapped students to interact with students who experience severe handicaps.

CLASSROOM ORGANIZATION, STRUCTURE, AND MATERIALS

Dividing the class into small heterogeneous groups facilitates interactions among students of various developmental levels to a greater degree than attempting to obtain interactions with larger groups (Nietupski, Hamre-Nietupski, Schuetz, & Ockwood, 1980; Taylor, 1982). Thus, it would appear that in order to help facilitate interactions between students with severe handicaps and nonhandicapped students, the teacher should arrange the classroom into small heterogeneous groups. For example, if a special education class of five students with

severe handicaps is joined with a regular education class of 25 nonhandicapped students to work on certain art projects or to participate in organized play activities, the teacher(s) should think in terms of dividing
the larger group of 30 students into smaller heterogeneous groups of
six students each with one handicapped student in each group. (This
illustration is meant to serve only as an example of how a classroom
might be organized.)

After the class is arranged into small heterogeneous groups, the
specific type of group structure used should be carefully considered.
The cooperative group structure described briefly in Chapter 2 could be
utilized. Researchers have found that the cooperative group structure
produces significantly more positive interactions between students with
handicaps and nonhandicapped students than either a competitive
or individualistic group structure (Rynders, Johnson, Johnson, &
Schmidt, 1980). As noted in Chapter 2, in the cooperative group
structure the group as a whole is assigned a common goal, and everyone
is encouraged to work together to reach the goal. In other words, if the
group's goal is to be reached, all students must coordinate their efforts
to achieve the goal. On the other hand, as noted by Johnson and
Johnson (1980), "when students are instructed to work alone with the
purpose of either outperforming their peers (competition) or meeting
a set criterion (individualistic learning), the initial tendency toward
the rejection of handicapped students is perpetuated and increased"
(p. 94). Arranging cooperative group structures is crucial. Thus, the
reader is encouraged to carefully review the work of researchers on
cooperative learning (Johnson & Johnson, 1980; Rynders, Johnson,
Johnson, & Schmidt, 1980).

Another classroom organization factor which has been found to
influence student interactions is the type of materials, toys, and
activities provided. Quiltich and Risley (1973) found that preschool-
age nonhandicapped children would play alone or together depending
on the materials and toys available. For example, during an organized
play period when materials such as wagons and balls were available,
the children interacted more often than when materials such as crayons
and puzzles were available. The latter, of course, can more readily
be used in isolated play. Stainback, Stainback, and Jaben (1981) have
related the implications of these and other similar findings specifically
to students with severe handicaps. They have observed that students
experiencing severe handicaps and nonhandicapped students also tend
to play together more frequently when social type toys are available.
This is especially true when both the students with severe handicaps and
nonhandicapped students know how to play with the toys. Stainback et
al. (1981) pointed out that the toys and materials selected to promote
social interaction should be age appropriate and challenging to both the
nonhandicapped students and students with severe handicaps.

A note of caution should be inserted here. After a careful analysis of the research related to the use of toys and materials to promote interactions, Strain and Kerr (1981) stated: "The manipulation of play materials as a singular intervention strategy is not likely to significantly change the isolated behavior of handicapped children" (p.26). Instead, they advocated that toys, games, and activities serve as only one tool for those employing procedures to promote interactions between students with handicaps and nonhandicapped students. Additional information about school and classroom organizational factors as well as a variety of materials that can be used to promote interactions are discussed later in Section V of this book.

In summary, an integrated classroom can be arranged to foster peer interactions between handicapped and nonhandicapped students. Factors that tend to facilitate interactions include (a) small heterogeneous group structuring; (b) a cooperative group goal orientation; and (c) the availability of materials and toys that promote socialization. Each of these factors can be used to complement the others in the arrangement of the integrated setting to foster desired peer interactions. See Table 1 for an overview of these considerations.

TRAINING NONHANDICAPPED STUDENTS

A second approach to promoting interactions is to train nonhandicapped students to interact with students who experience severe handicaps. One of the main rationales for this approach is that research has shown that in integrated situations, some nonhandicapped students

TABLE 1
Organization, Structure and Material Considerations
for Promoting Interactions

Considerations	Good	Poor
Organization	Small, heterogeneous groupings	Large homogeneous groups or individual work areas
Structure	Cooperative goals	Competitive or individualistic goals
Materials	Social type (e.g. ball, wagon)	Isolate type (e.g. puzzle, crayons)

are nonaccepting of students with severe handicaps. Also, some nonhandicapped students have been found to reject or to be cruel to students with handicaps in integrated situations (Jones, 1972). Therefore, teachers wishing to promote interactions between students with severe handicaps and nonhandicapped students may need to modify the attitudes and interactional behaviors of nonhandicapped students toward their peers with severe handicaps.

The need to train nonhandicapped students is based on the premise that if nonhandicapped students are nonaccepting of or cruel to handicapped students, we should work to change their attitudes and behaviors. In other words, such attitudes and behaviors represent a problem belonging to nonhandicapped students. We do not want them growing up to be adults who are unaccepting of or cruel to handicapped persons. Some professionals have begun to develop procedures, activities, and materials for training nonhandicapped students. A discussion of training procedures and activities and materials that could be used in a training program are included in Sections III and V of this book.

In summary, training nonhandicapped students to interact with students who have severe handicaps may be a necessary complement to our programming efforts to facilitate successful integration. Thus, regular and special class teachers may want to train nonhandicapped students in how to approach and interact in positive ways with students who experience severe handicaps.

TRAINING STUDENTS WITH SEVERE HANDICAPS

A third approach to promoting positive interactions between students with severe handicaps and nonhandicapped students is to focus on enhancing the social skills of the students with severe handicaps (Gaylord-Ross, et al, 1984). The rationale here is that the more appropriate social skills handicapped students possess, the more nonhandicapped students will tend to interact with them. Thus, special classroom teachers should work, in cooperation with regular class teachers, to help build the social skills of students experiencing severe handicaps.

A variety of procedures has been used to teach social skills to students with severe handicaps. An in-depth presentation of assessment and instructional strategies for teaching social interaction skills to handicapped students is presented in Section IV of this book.

CONCLUSION

In this chapter, three basic approaches have been delineated which could be incorporated into integrated classrooms or other situations to facilitate interactions between students with severe handicaps and nonhandicapped students. These are: (a) the systematic design and arrangement of classroom organization, structure, and materials; (b) the incorporation of instructional programs designed to train and motivate nonhandicapped students to interact with students who experience severe handicaps; and (c) the implementation of procedures to train students with severe handicaps in socialization skills.

Finally, it should be reiterated that it is becoming increasingly apparent that the mere physical placement of students with severe handicaps in the educational mainstream may not meet the goal of meaningful social integration. Physical placement coupled with the systematic implementation of procedures to promote positive social interactions appears to be needed (Schutz, Williams, Iverson, & Duncan, 1984; Taylor, 1982).

REFERENCES

Faught, K., Balleweg, B., Crow, R., & Van Den Pol, R. (1983). An analysis of social behaviors among handicapped and nonhandicapped preschool children. *Education and Training of the Mentally Retarded, 18*, 210-214.

Gaylord-Ross, R., Haring, T., Breen, C., & Pitts-Conway, U. (1984). The training and generalization of social interaction skills with autistic youth. *Journal of Applied Behavior Analysis, 17*, 229-247.

Guralnick, M. (1980). Social interactions among preschool children. *Exceptional Children, 46*, 248-253.

Johnson, D., & Johnson, R. (1980). Integrating handicapped students into the mainstream. *Exceptional Children, 47*, 90-98.

Jones, R. (1972). Labels and stigma in special education. *Exceptional Children, 38*, 553-564.

Nietupski, J., Hamre-Nietupski, S., Schuetz, G., & Ockwood, L. (Eds.) (1980). *Severely handicapped students in regular schools.* Milwaukee: Milwaukee Public Schools.

Quilitch, H. R., & Risley, T. R. (1973). The effects of play materials on social play. *Journal of Applied Behavior Analysis, 6*, 573-578.

Rynders, J., Johnson, R., Johnson, D., & Schmidt, B. (1980). Producing positive interaction among Down syndrome and nonhandicapped teenagers through cooperative goal structuring. *American Journal of Mental Deficiency, 85*, 268-283.

Schutz, R., Williams, W., Iverson, G., & Duncan, D. (1984). Social integration of severely handicapped students. In N. Certo, N. Haring, & R. York (Eds.), *Public School Integration of Severely Handicapped Students.* Baltimore: Paul Brookes.

Stainback, W., Stainback, S., & Jaben, T. (1981). Providing opportunities for interaction between severely handicapped and nonhandicapped students. *Teaching Exceptional Children, 13*, 72-75.

Strain, P., & Kerr, M. (1981). Modifying children's social withdrawal: Issues in assessment and clinical intervention. In M. Hersen, R. Eisler, & P. Miller (Eds.), *Progress in behavior modification* (Vol. II). New York: Academic Press.

Taylor, S. (1982). From segregation to integration: Strategies for integrating severely handicapped students in normal school and community settings. *Journal of the Association for the Severely Handicapped, 8*, 42-49.

Section III

Educating
Nonhandicapped Students

Chapter 6

Rationale for Educating Nonhandicapped Students

One possible way to encourage or promote interactions would be to educate nonhandicapped students about students who experience severe handicaps. The purpose of this chapter is to provide an in-depth rationale for why educating nonhandicapped students could lead to increased positive interaction between students with severe handicaps and nonhandicapped students in integrated settings.

SOCIAL PREFERENCE BEHAVIORS

When the interaction behavior of nonhandicapped students and students experiencing severe handicaps has been carefully analyzed in integrated free play situations, nonhandicapped students show a definite preference for interacting with other nonhandicapped or mildly handicapped students rather than with severely handicapped students. On the other hand, students with severe handicaps display no consistent preference for interacting with students experiencing mild or severe handicaps or nonhandicapped peers. For example, Guralnick (1980) summarized the results of a study he conducted in an integrated setting with students of varying developmental levels:

> NH (non-handicapped) and Mi (mildly-handicapped) groups communicated with each other significantly more than expected by the criterion of availability and considerably less with Mo (moderately-handicapped) and S (severely-handicapped) children. Moderately and severely handicapped children, on the other hand, communicated with all groups generally in accordance with their availability....Moreover, the change that occurred from pre-testing essentially served to enhance this basic pattern. (p. 251)

Since students with severe handicaps have no preference for interacting with students of different developmental levels, it is possible that students with severe handicaps would interact with nonhandicapped students if nonhandicapped students would interact with them. There is some research to support this supposition. When researchers have trained nonhandicapped students to increase their positive social behaviors toward students with severe handicaps, they have found that not only did the nonhandicapped students increase their social behavior toward students with severe handicaps, but also that the students with severe handicaps displayed increased social behavior toward the nonhandicapped students who were positive toward them (Strain, Shores, & Timm, 1977).

LIMITATIONS OF FOCUSING ALL TRAINING ON HANDICAPPED STUDENTS

Strain and Kerr (1981) have pointed out that "children's characteristic social behaviors set the occasion for predictable peer consequences" (p.5). That is, the passive, withdrawn, or clumsy and socially inept child is seldom the recipient of positive social initiations by peers, while the competent, socially astute, active youngster is often sought for interactions. Unfortunately, research tends to indicate that teachers and/or nonhandicapped peers (acting as change agents) have difficulty fostering durable and generalizable positive, high-level social skills in students experiencing severe handicaps. Therefore, it may be important to train nonhandicapped students to interact with students who are not highly competent and socially active or who may not show even "acceptable" levels of social skills.

While all students should be trained to have the most desirable social skills possible, some students with severe handicaps in integrated settings will probably show marked deficits in social as well as academic skills. If they become highly competent and socially astute, they probably will no longer be labeled as students experiencing severe handicaps. Rather than take the position that these students should be excluded from integrated experiences until they show "acceptable" levels of social skills so as to avoid being ignored or rejected by their nonhandicapped peers, it appears logical to train nonhandicapped students to interact with students with severe handicaps who may not, in all cases, be considered highly competent and socially astute.

The authors are not stating that the social skills of students with severe handicaps cannot be improved. In fact, it is probable that training the nonhandicapped to interact with students with severe handicaps will indirectly improve the social skills of severely handicapped students. The reason is that if nonhandicapped students interact with them, the severely handicapped students will receive practice and experience in interacting with nonhandicapped students. However, while improvement in the socialization skills of students with severe handicaps is imperative and can be made (see Gaylord-Ross, et al, 1984 and Chapters 9 and 10), it may not be possible in all instances for handicapped students to become the highly competent and socially astute individuals alluded to by Strain & Kerr (1981) as being needed to "set the occasion" to naturally elicit positive responses from others. Thus, training nonhandicapped students to interact with students who experience severe handicaps may be necessary, since many students with severe handicaps do not display "high level" social behaviors.

FEASIBILITY OF TRAINING NONHANDICAPPED STUDENTS

A study by McHale and Simeonsson (1980) has provided a clear "cue" that training nonhandicapped students to interact with students with severe handicaps has a good probability of meeting with success. As part of a larger study, McHale and Simeonsson measured nonhandicapped students' "understandings" of the problems of a group of students with severe handicaps (elementary age students labeled autistic confounded by mental retardation). They also examined the relationship of this "understanding" to the behavior of nonhandicapped students toward students with severe handicaps and found that the nonhandicapped students' "understandings" were positively related to the frequency of their communication with handicapped students. McHale and Simeonsson concluded that "the findings that positive behavior toward autistic peers was related to children's previous understanding about handicapped peers indicates the need to educate young children about handicapped children" (p. 23).

Many of the behaviors (e.g., academic, social, attitudinal) of nonhandicapped individuals can be changed through systematic instructional techniques and procedures. Therefore, if nonhandicapped students should show reluctance or hesitation toward interacting with students who experience severe handicaps, educators should be challenged to train nonhandicapped students to display more positive behaviors and attitudes toward these students. In short, if interactions between the students with severe handicaps and nonhandicapped students are desired, it appears feasible to train the nonhandicapped to emit the behaviors that will foster the desired interactions.

CONCLUSION

While a combination of several methods may be necessary to achieve the goal of interaction between students with severe handicaps and nonhandicapped students, educating nonhandicapped students about students with severe handicaps is one method that should receive some attention. In recent years, materials and activities for sensitizing nonhandicapped students to students with severe handicaps have been developed. (See Chapter 13 for a review of some of these.)

REFERENCES

Guralnick, M. H. (1980).   Social interactions among preschool children. *Exceptional Children, 46*, 248-253.

McHale, S. M., & Simeonsson, R. J. (1980).   Effects of interaction on handicapped children's attitudes toward autistic children. *American Journal of Mental Deficiency, 85*, 18-24.

Strain, P., & Kerr, M. (1981). Modifying children's social withdrawal: Issues in assessment and clinical intervention. In M. Hersen, R. Eilser, & P. Miller

(Eds.), *Progress in behavior modification* Vol. II. New York: Academic Press.

Strain, P. S., Shores, R. E. & Timm, M. A. (1977). Effects of peer social initiations on the behavior of withdrawn preschool children. *Journal of Applied Behavior Analysis, 10*, 289-298.

Gaylord-Ross, R., Haring, T., Breen, C., & Pitts-Conway, U. (1984). The training and generalization of social interaction skills with autistic youth. *Journal of Applied Behavior Analysis, 17*, 229-247.

Chapter 7

Assessment for Program Planning and Evaluation

In the previous chapter, the importance of educating nonhandicapped students about their severely handicapped peers was discussed. However, before developing and implementing a training program, it is essential to first assess nonhandicapped students' knowledge of and attitudes and behaviors toward students with severe handicaps. This is the only way to determine exactly what information and experiences should be included in a training program. In addition, once the program is implemented, it is important to engage in ongoing assessment of the progress being made; that is, whether or not the training program is being successful.

In this chapter, the assessment of nonhandicapped students' knowledge of and attitudes and behaviors toward students with severe handicaps is discussed. The intent is not to provide standardized instruments for assessment but rather to provide guidelines for the development of teacher-made assessment tools designed to meet the needs of a particular set of students and situation. The chapter is divided into two major sections covering (a) what type of knowledge, attitudes, and behaviors should be assessed and (b) guidelines for the development of assessment tools.

WHAT TO ASSESS

An initial step in any assessment procedure involves determining what data are relevant to the purpose or objective of the assessment. A few suggestions about what to assess are offered here.

In regard to *knowledge*, it is important to determine whether nonhandicapped students know how to communicate with a nonverbal peer, how to adapt games or groups activities so students who cannot remember all the rules, or who cannot jump, speak, or see can participate, how to adjust a wheelchair, and/or when not to help a peer perform a task or part of a task. However, it is usually *not* necessary to assess nonhandicapped students' knowledge about definitions of handicapping conditions, categories of exceptionality, incidence figures, and various syndromes. Such information is of little or no value in day-to-day interactions with their handicapped peers; thus, whether or not nonhandicapped students possess such information is of little practical value in terms of nonhandicapped students and students with severe handicaps playing and/or working together.

Attitudes involve how students feel or what they believe. It is often useful to know how nonhandicapped students feel about, for example, working, playing and eating lunch with a particular student who is nonambulatory and/or who cannot keep up or comprehend all of what is being said or done. On the other hand, attempting to measure nonhandicapped students' attitudes toward students with severe handicaps as a homogeneous group often yields data that is at best confusing. This was clarified to the authors by a third grade student who when asked, "Do you like to play with severely handicapped students at recess?" responded by insightfully asking, "Which one?" Thus, when measuring attitudes it is generally more useful to focus on attitudes toward individual persons, and their characteristics and behaviors, rather than the category of students with "severe handicaps." Also, from a sociometric perspective of students attitudes toward their peers,the concept of acceptance and rejection require consideration. For example, as Carlson, Lahey and Neeper (1984) pointed out, a lack of selection or nomination as a friend, playmate or work partner may indicate a category of students who are neglected or isolates rather than rejected by their peers. Similarly, Asher and Taylor (1981) have noted that while it is common for acceptance scales to ask students to list their friends, there is a distinct difference between friendship and acceptance in group situations. That is, a peer can be accepted but not be considered a friend. Thus care must be exercised to interpret attitude data correctly.

The most critical and useful data is the *behavior* nonhandicapped students actually exhibit in integration activities with students who experience severe handicaps. After all, it is behavior change that is the ultimate objective. Thus, the best indication regarding needed training and/or the success of training efforts can be gleaned from the amount and types of interactions nonhandicapped students actually display toward students with severe handicaps. Also important is whether nonhandicapped students use adapted equipment appropriately and whether they successfully include their peers with severe handicaps in games and group activities.

In summary, it is important to carefully consider exactly what to assess in the areas of knowledge, attitudes, and behaviors. Otherwise, the data gathered may be confusing or of little practical value. Furthermore, choosing or designing an assessment device will depend on what information you want to collect.

Finally, it should be stressed here that when looking at people as individuals, regardless of the types of assessment tools used for gathering data, care must be exercised to ensure that we do not single out a particular student. This could cause embarrassment for the student as well as possibly causing the peers of the student to wonder what is "wrong" with him or her. It could inadvertently lead to a widening of the social gap between the student and his or her peers. This does not mean that you cannot ask specific questions about a specific student. However, whenever questions are asked about a particular student, questions should be asked about a number of students, so not to single out one or a few individuals. Also, the students being asked about should represent a wide range of characteristics (e.g., popularity, achievement, athletic skill, handicapped and nonhandicapped, etc.). In addition to decreasing the chance of widening the social gap between the student(s) being asked about and the general school population, the data collected can serve as comparison data as to the breadth of discrepancy in attitudes toward, for example, a severely handicapped student and a variety of his or her peers.

ASSESSMENT TOOLS

There are a number of assessment tools teachers could use to collect data on nonhandicapped students' knowledge of and attitudes and behaviors toward students with severe handicaps. Three commonly used assessment tools are reviewed here: (a) the questionnaire, (b) the interview, and (c) direct observation.

Questionnaire

A questionnaire is a series of questions aimed at gathering specific information. Questionnaires are typically in a paper-and-pencil format and are generally administered on a group basis. They are particularly suited for collecting basic knowledge and attitude type data.

Questionnaires can be developed in either a closed or open format. The closed type, in which the respondents must choose a predetermined option, simplifies compilation and analysis of the data; however, the open type, in which respondents develop their own answers, allows for potentially greater accuracy in understanding a respondent's depth of knowledge or range of views. Several examples of different types of questionnaire items are listed in Table 1.

Questionnaires can be designed to meet the needs of respondents of widely ranging abilities. For nonreaders, picture sequences can be used to depict questions and choices. For students with attention difficulties, questions can be presented one at a time and/or individually explained if necessary. Flexibility to meet the needs of respondents and efficiency in

TABLE 1
Examples of Questionnaire Items

A. *Pictorial Item for Nonreaders*—preschool/elementary level
   1. Do you like to play with any of these students? (Read by teacher)

picture of student named	playing

     Circle One: (Read by teacher)

       yes   maybe   no

B. *Open-Ended Item Sequence*—elementary level
   1. Do you like to play with any of the students who you share recess period*
      with?
   2. If so, which ones and why?
   3. Which ones would you not like to play with and why?
      *includes, for example, class for students with severe handicaps and a third grade class.

C. *Forced Choice*—elementary level
   1. Would you like to have recess with the students
      in Miss Jones'* class?   Always   Sometimes   Never
   2. Would you like to have recess with the students
      in Miss Smith's** class?   Always   Sometimes   Never
      *Class for students with severe handicaps. **Class of students in the regular fourth grade.

D. *Pictorial Item*—secondary level
   1. What kind of activities would you like to do with each of these students?
      (Teacher reads)

Student No. 1's Picture	Choose One:			
		Talking and/or doing things together	Being at the same game or activity	Nothing

E. *Open Ended Question*—secondary level
   1. How does being around (Steve Jones) make you feel?
   2. Why?
      (Repeat sequence with other students' names, some handicapped and
      some not.)

F. *Forced Choice*—secondary level
   1. Would you be willing to have Steve Jones as a partner on
      the school clean-up committee?   Yes Maybe No
   2. Would you be willing to have Steve Jones as a participant
      in the junior/senior follies?   Yes Maybe No
   3. Do you think Steve Jones should have his picture in the
      yearbook?   Yes Maybe No
      (Repeat sequence with other students' names, some handicapped and
      some not.)

collecting a wide range of data from a variety of students are advantages inherent in the use of questionnaires.

Borg (1981) and Borg and Gall (1979) have suggested guidelines for the development of a questionnaire. Some of the most important points are reviewed here.

1. Clarity of the items is essential. In order to gather meaningful data, the items or questions must be interpreted correctly by the respondents. Thus, it is important to avoid terms like "several" or "some" that have no precise meaning. Giving a pretest of the items to a few randomly selected respondents is one way to locate potential ambiguities.

2. It is important to avoid biased or leading questions. Search out and eliminate or modify questions that may bias or lead the respondents toward a particular answer. For example, if a question unintentionally gives a cue regarding what the teacher wants, the students might respond accordingly rather than selecting or providing their own answers. Having a colleague or several colleagues critically read a draft copy of the questionnaire could help reduce the chances of this problem occurring.

3. Avoid questions that may be threatening. The teacher should try to put him/herself into the respondent's position to determine whether an answer may be perceived as threatening. Also, it should be made clear to the respondents that the answers given on the questionnaire will not be counted for or against them in any way. The purpose is only to find out what they know or think.

4. Keep all items short and simple. This usually makes the questions easier to understand. Including more than one idea or a very complex idea within one question may confuse or make it difficult for respondents to accurately interpret the questions.

5. Generally speaking, try to avoid negative items. These are frequently misread and result in an answer that is opposite from the respondent's true intentions.

6. Ask questions that involve information the respondents are likely to know about. If, for example, nonhandicapped students are not familiar with or do not know a nonverbal peer who is slow to comprehend what is going on around him or her, they cannot be expected to answer questions about this characterisitic of some students in any meaningful way.

7. In order to check whether the questionnaire accurately reflects the attitudes or knowledge base of the respondents, a follow-up interview with a few randomly selected students can be done.

Interview

An interview is a tool for collecting data through direct verbal interaction. It is sometimes referred to as an oral questionnaire (Borg, 1981). Like the questionnaire, it is commonly used to assess knowledge and attitudes.

However, there are some distinct differences. An interview can be used to elicit in-depth information regarding the topic of concern. In an interview, the teacher is not restricted only to asking questions but has the opportunity to clarify, refine, and probe further when needed to gain a better understanding of what an individual thinks or knows. Two examples of interview sequences are listed in Table 2.

Interviews can be formal or informal in nature. While the formal interview is the procedure typically used, teachers also have available the option of questioning a respondent regarding his or her attitudes or knowledge on an informal basis when a situation occurs in which immediate questioning could be potentially insightful. However, interviewing also has some disadvantages. Because interviews are usually conducted on a one-to-one basis, they are considerably more time consuming. For this reason, interviewing has often been used to validate and delve more deeply into information gleaned from initial questionnaire data collected. Also, as a result of the face-to-face contact, respondents may not respond candidly to the questions posed for fear of a negative perception being formed by the teacher (or interviewer) based on the answer given.

There are guidelines that should be followed when preparing for and conducting an interview. A few of the most salient are reviewed here.

1. The objectives or purposes of an interview should be clearly delineated. Exactly what information is desired should be clear to the teacher. It is best to put into a written statement the objectives of the interview.

2. The development of an interview guide is useful in order to increase consistency of questioning and keep the interviewer focused toward obtaining the information desired. An interview guide is a written series of questions that the teacher intends to ask. Along with the questions, the sequence for asking the questions and notes regarding additional probes that may be helpful can be included.

3. Questions to be asked during the interview should be constructed and evaluated in light of the concerns previously noted regarding questionnaire items. For example, leading, negatively stated, and/or threatening questions should be avoided.

4. A data-recording procedure shold be established before beginning. A tape recorder is suggested to obtain the most accurate and complete record. However, some interviewees may be uncomfortable with this procedure, or a tape recorder may not be available. If the

TABLE 2
Examples of Interview Sequences

A. Preschool/Early Elementary Sequence

Q. Do you like to play with (student's name)?
A. No, me and my friends don't like her.

Q. Why don't you like her?
A. I just don't. Nobody does.

Q. Is it because she is not very good at playing the games you like?
A. No, lots of kids are good and bad at playing some games.

Q. Is it because she cannot walk or talk very well?
A. No, we usually know what she wants and we can push her wheelchair wherever she needs to be.

Q. Then why don't you like her?
A. Because she is a tattletale and lies and always gets us in trouble with the teacher and she will not take turns and be fair. She cries when she doesn't get her own way too. We don't like her around when we are playing.

B. Secondary Age Sequence

Q. Would you be willing to work in shop class with (student's name) as your building partner?
A. I would rather not.

Q. Could you tell me why?
A. I'm not sure.

Q. Do you think that he can't do the job and would ruin your chance for having a good project?
A. No, he is real good with tools and is dependable.

Q. Does he have poor personal habits like being smelly or dirty?
A. No, he is clean. He doesn't dress too good, sort of like a "nerd," you know.

Q. Well, would you be uncomfortable because the other guys will ride you for having a special education student as a shop partner?
A. Sure they will, but I can handle that. But the main problem is that he makes me uncomfortable.

Q. How does he make you uncomfortable?
A. I feel real guilty because I can walk and talk good and he can't. I get embarrassed when I can't understand him or the other guys make fun of him.

TABLE 2 *Continued*

Q. Is there anything else that makes you uncomfortable?
A. Well, I am sort of afraid of him. If I can't understand him or if I hassle him he might get mad. I would if I were him. He is really a big guy. So, you see I really don't want to be his partner.

---

interviewer takes notes on what is said, attention to accuracy and completeness are important to get as clear a picture as possible. The interviewer may want to review his or her notes after the interview is over to add to the notes or fill in gaps.

5. Finally, and perhaps most important, the interviewer should possess the ability to develop rapport with and sensitivity toward the interviewee. If trust and understanding are not present in the interview relationship, the extensiveness and validity of any data collected may be reduced.

In summary, in situations where the teacher wants to know the reasons for actions, feelings, and attitudes, the interview can be most effective. In the hands of a skillful teacher, a depth of response is possible—that is, a penetration quite unlikely to be achieved through any other means.

Direct Observation

Since one of the purposes of educating nonhandicapped students about students with severe handicaps is to enhance the frequency of the nonhandicapped students' positive interactions with them, teachers will need to keep measures on the number and types of interactions that occur before, during, and after the educational program for the nonhandicapped is implemented. School personnel can assess nonhandicapped students' interactions with students who experience severe handicaps by observing nonhandicapped students in play or work situations with handicapped students and simply recording their interactions. An example of an interaction observation recording sheet is provided in Table 3. The operational definitions of the coding symbols used on the recording sheet are included in Table 4.

TABLE 3
Example of Interaction Observation Recording Sheet

Interaction Observation Recording Sheet
for Preschool Integrated Play Activities

Student's Name and/or Number_____Date_____Time_____

Classification: SH NH Sex: M F Setting_____

Directions: Circle the appropriate symbols at or during a predesignated observation time (e.g., every 20 seconds). If the target student is engaging in a social interaction, circle "SI" on Item 1, Activity, and then circle the appropriate descriptors of the interaction in Items 2 through 7. If the target subject is not engaging in a social interaction, circle "NSI" on Item 1, Activity, and then circle the appropriate descriptor of the student's activity only on Item 8, Noninteraction. Only one circle per item should be made. (See Table 4 for operational definitions of the symbols used.)

Observation Interval #_____	Observation Interval #_____
1. Activity SI NSI	1. Activity SI NSI
2. Size IN GP	2. Size IN GP
3. Type V/V Phy Vis TC	3. Type V/V Phy Vis TC
4. Partner SH NH OT PC	4. Partner SH NH OT PC
5. Sex of Partner M F SC	5. Sex of Partner M F SC
6. Student's Role I R C	6. Student's Role I R C
7. Student's Affect P Nu N	7. Student's Affect P Nu N
8. Noninteraction PP IP I	8. Noninteraction PP IP I

Observation Interval #_____	Observation Interval #_____
1. Activity SI NSI	1. Activity SI NSI
2. Size IN GP	2. Size IN GP
3. Type V/V Phy Vis TC	3. Type V/V Phy Vis TC
4. Partner SH NH OT PC	4. Partner SH NH OT PC
5. Sex of Partner M F SC	5. Sex of Partner M F SC
6. Student's Role I R C	6. Student's Role I R C
7. Student's Affect P Nu N	7. Student's Affect P Nu N
8. Noninteraction PP IP I	8. Noninteraction PP IP I

Observation Interval #_____	Observation Interval #_____
1. Activity SI NSI	1. Activity SI NSI
2. Size IN GP	2. Size IN GP
3. Type V/V Phy Vis TC	3. Type V/V Phy Vis TC
4. Partner SH NH OT PC	4. Partner SH NH OT PC
5. Sex of Partner M F SC	5. Sex of Partner M F SC
6. Student's Role I R C	6. Student's Role I R C
7. Student's Affect P Nu N	7. Student's Affect P Nu N
8. Noninteraction PP IP I	8. Noninteraction PP IP I

TABLE 4
Operational Definitions for Interaction Observation Recording Sheet

1. Activity	*SI* =	Social interaction, interchange between two or more individuals in which target student is involved
	NSI =	Target student is *not* involved in an interchange with another individual
2. Size	*IN* =	Interacting with one individual
	GP =	Interacting with more than one individual simultaneously
3. Type	*V/V* =	Verbalization or vocalization interaction
	Phy =	Physical interaction in which touching between the interactors occurs (includes contact through objects)
	Vis =	Visual social exchange in which neither touching nor verbalization/vocalizations are involved
	TC =	Combination of at least two of the predesignated types occurs simultaneously
4. Partner	*SH* =	Peer with a severe handicap, as predetermined by teacher/investigator
	NH =	Peer without severe handicap, as predetermined by teacher/investigator
	OT =	Other; anyone other than student peers; e.g., teacher, aide, parent, etc.
	PC =	Partner combination, at least two of predesignated partner groups involved
5. Sex of Partner	*M* =	Male
	F =	Female
	SC =	Combination of both sexes in group
6. Student's Role	*I* =	Target student is the active initiator in the interaction exchange
	R =	Target student is a receiver of an interaction
	C =	Both the target student and another are initiating simultaneously
7. Student's Affect	*P* =	Positive; target student is exhibiting behaviors indicative of liking such as smiling, laughing, or verbalizing enjoyment

Continued on next page

TABLE 4 *Continued*

	Nu =	Neutral; target student is exhibiting behaviors indicative of contentment or comfort but not definitely positive or negative
	N =	Negative; target student is exhibiting behaviors indicative of dislike, such as crying, frowning, and/or verbal statements of dislike
8. Noninteraction	*PP* =	Parallel play, corresponding play activity occurs in which no interaction between individuals occurs; e.g., two students playing with the same set of trucks in close proximity in the same way without one acknowledging the other
	IP =	Isolated play; target student is playing by him/herself
	I =	Isolation; target student is not interacting with either others or materials, not acknowledging the external environment

Teachers can develop their own observational instruments to assess the behaviors nonhandicapped students exhibit in integration activities with students who have severe handicaps. Several guidelines to follow are suggested in this section to assist school personnel in the development of direct observational instruments.

1. Select and operationally define the target behaviors deemed pertinent for measurement. The behaviors selected for observation should be relevant; that is, functional to integration activities that normally occur. Once the most critical behaviors requiring attention have been identified, each behavior needs to be defined in observable terms. Definitions must be stated so that whether the behavior being observed is or is not occurring can be clearly and accurately determined. If a behavior is nonrelevant or if the definition is open to interpretation, the usefulness and/or accuracy of the data obtained may be questionable.

2. Once the behavior(s) to be measured is(are) selected and defined, the type of recording technique that can most accurately reflect the amount and changes in the chosen behavior(s) should be determined. Behavior may be counted to provide a *frequency* or timed to provide a *duration*. The type of behavior selected and/or the

situation may influence this choice. For example, nonhandicapped students' play behaviors with students who experience severe handicaps may be more meaningfully measured by how *much* time they spend playing with students who experience severe handicaps than how *many* times. That is, a nonhandicapped student may only play once with a student with a severe handicap during a recess period, but it lasts the entire period. Data may also be collected on whether the behavior of concern occurred or did not occur during a particular time period (interval) or at certain points in time (momentary time sampling).

3. Another suggestion is to determine and construct a means to record data collected on the target behaviors being observed. Accuracy in recording the data being collected is as critical a concern as specifying and defining the behaviors and determining an appropriate recording technique. If the data is not recorded accurately, the findings of the analysis of the data may provide a distorted picture that does not reflect what really happened in the integration setting between the nonhandicapped students and students with severe handicaps. Data recording methods such as paper and pencil coding sheets, wrist counters, stopwatches, and tape recorders have all been used in various combinations of ways to record the behaviors observed. The method(s) determined most appropriate for use in a given situation should be what is easiest and quickest for the observer to use while maintaining maximal accuracy.

4. It is generally most appropriate to collect direct observational data in an integrated (nonhandicapped students and students with severe handicaps) free play or joint work activity period in which both the regular and special teacher are present. With two teachers present, one can observe and the other can supervise.

5. Preparation time is usually necessary. The individual(s) serving as the observer(s) should engage in practice sessions until they become proficient in the use of and comfortable with the definitions of behaviors, recording techniques, and methods.

6. Finally, interrater reliability of the direct observational tool or instrument should be determined prior to data collection. Also, a colleague should be requested to periodically do interrater reliability checks to monitor the reliability of the instrument throughout its use.

Direct observation provides a means to assess the most critical variable of concern; that is, the actual behavior exhibited by a nonhandicapped student in an integrated setting with peers who experience severe handicaps. However, while providing the most critical assessment data, direct observation is generally the most time consuming of the three procedures discussed. The reader is referred to the sources listed at the end of the chapter for more detailed information about questionnaires, interviews, direct observation, and other assessment and evaluation procedures and tools.

CONCLUSION

As noted in the introduction, when contemplating the development of a training program to educate nonhandicapped students, it is essential to first assess nonhandicapped students' knowledge of as well as attitudes and behaviors toward their peers with severe handicaps. This is the only way to determine if an educational program to train nonhandicapped students is, in fact, needed. Also, if a training program is needed, additional data collection is essential to ascertain (a) what information and experiences to include in the training program and (b) whether or not the program, when implemented, actually results in the desired change(s).

When developing assessment instruments, it is sometimes helpful to review instruments that others have developed. McHale and Simeonsson (1980), Stainback and Stainback (1982), and Voeltz (1980, 1982) have reported research in which they used various assessment instruments to measure the attitudes and/or knowledge of nonhandicapped students about students with severe handicaps. Nietupski, Stainback, Gleissner, Stainback, and Hamre-Nietupski (1983) and Strain, Kerr, and Ragland (1979) have reported research in which they used direct observational instruments to measure the social behaviors between nonhandicapped students and students with severe handicaps. The reader may want to review one or more of these reports.

Finally, it should be noted that while data collection may involve either individual or group procedures, the analysis of the data should be handled on an individual, per student basis. Just as it has been pointed out that each student who exhibits a severe handicap is an individual with his or her own unique characteristics, so too, is each nonhandicapped student unique. Group analysis of nonhandicapped students' knowledge, behaviors, and attitudes can potentially result in misrepresentation of the training needs of any individual student in the group. There are wide variations among nonhandicapped students and the development of a training program for nonhandicapped students based on group averages, rather than individual data, may not suffice.

REFERENCES

Asher, S., & Taylor, A. (1981). Social outcomes of mainstreaming: Sociometric assessment and beyond. *Exceptional Education Quarterly, 1*, 13-30.

Borg, W. (1981). *Applying educational research.* New York: Longman.

Borg, W., & Gall, M. (1979). *Educational research.* New York: Longman.

Carlson, C., Lahey, B., & Neeper, R. (1984). Peer assessment of the social behavior of accepted, rejected and neglected children. *Journal of Abnormal Child Psychology, 12,* 189-198.

McHale, S., & Simeonsson, R. (1980). Effects of interaction on non-handicapped children's attitudes toward autistic children. *American Journal of Mental Deficiency, 85,* 18-24.

Nietupski, S., Stainback, W., Gleissner, L., Stainback, S., & Hamre-Nietupski, S. (1983). Effects of socially outgoing versus withdrawn peer partners on nonhandicapped-handicapped student interaction. *Behavioral Disorders, 8,* 244-250.

Stainback, S., & Stainback, W. (1982). Non-handicapped students' perceptions of severely handicapped students. *Education and Training of the Mentally Retarded, 17,* 177-182.

Strain, P., Kerr, M., & Ragland, E. (1979). Effects of peer-mediated social initiations and prompting/reinforcement procedures on social behavior of autistic children. *Journal of Autism and Developmental Disorders, 9,* 42-54.

Voeltz, L. (1980). Children's attitudes toward handicapped peers. *American Journal of Mental Deficiency, 84,* 455-464.

Voeltz, L. (1982). Effects of structured interactions with severely handicapped peers on children's attitudes. *American Journal of Mental Deficiency, 86,* 380-389.

Chapter 8

A Model for Educating Nonhandicapped Students

For the first time in their lives, many nonhandicapped students are coming into direct contact with students who have severe handicaps. How nonhandicapped students react to students with severe handicaps could be critical to the success of the integration movement.

While the majority of nonhandicapped students have been found to hold positive attitudes toward students' with severe handicaps (Stainback & Stainback, 1982; Voeltz, 1980), it has been observed, unfortunately, that there are some nonhandicapped students who display behaviors indicative of rejection, disgust, fear, anxiety, and, perhaps even worse, pity in the presence of their peers with severe handicaps (Burton & Hirshoren, 1979). Thus, educators should attempt to influence the education of nonhandicapped students to ensure that as many of them as possible react in a positive and accepting manner to their peers with severe handicaps. As Voeltz (1980) stated:

> Even if researchers were to document that some non-handicapped children exhibit an intolerance for their handicapped peers that includes a willingness to engage in overtly cruel behavior, this should posit a challenge to educators rather than a limitation. Surely such behavior of presumably "normal" children is as susceptible to change as the behavior of severely handicapped children, now apparently acquiring skills once thought unattainable. (p. 463)

The purpose of this chapter is to present a training sequence model for educating nonhandicapped students about students with severe handicaps. While there are a growing number of instructional materials (see Chapter 13) available for teaching nonhandicapped students about individual differences, there is a paucity of information in regard to an organized training sequence for teaching nonhandicapped students about individual differences.

There are two major components contained in the proposed training model. These components are (a) classroom instruction, and (b) guided experiences. See Figure 1 for a visual representation of the model.

The proposed model, based on the practical experiences of professionals who have worked with individual differences training in the schools and on the available professional literature related to individual differences training, is designed to provide one sequence for training nonhandicapped students to interact positively with handicapped students. The instructional component of the model is discussed first. An explanation of the guided experiences component follows.

INSTRUCTIONAL COMPONENT

Instruction in the classroom setting focuses on fostering cognitive awareness and understanding of the concepts inherent in human differences training.   Instructional concerns include recognition of similarities, understanding differences, and dealing with differences.

FIGURE 1
Human Differences Training Sequence

Program Components	*Instruction*	*Guided Experiences*
Level 1	Recognition of similarities among people	Experiences that capitalize on similarities among individuals
Level 2	Cognitive understanding of human differences	Experiences that foster an understanding of differences
Level 3	Knowledge of strategies to deal with differences	Supervised use of strategies to deal with differences
Desired Product	Nonhandicapped students who have the knowledge and experiences that will enable them to interact with, advocate for, and educate others to be sensitive to and respect human differences.	

Recognition of Similarities

As a result of the severity of the handicapping condition(s) exhibited by many students with severe handicaps, most nonhandicapped peers quickly recognize differences in this population. Too often, these differences are so foreign and overpowering to the nonhandicapped students they interfere with the recognition of similarities between themselves and their peers who experience severe handicaps (Cummings, 1974). Because of this lack of understanding, some nonhandicapped students may experience discomfort or even fear in the presence of individuals with severe handicaps.

It could be hypothesized that such irrational discomfort and fear results from uncorrected ignorance (Donaldson, 1980). A first step is to teach students to recognize that individuals with severe handicaps are people just like themselves. Recognition that students with severe handicaps have feelings, emotions, likes, and dislikes is important to a basic cognitive acceptance of each of these students as a fellow citizen (human being).

Recognition of similarities can most easily begin on a concrete level with the recognition of similarities in simple basic needs. At more advanced stages more abstract similarities can be recognized, such as preferences (e.g., liking peanut butter but disliking spinach), and feelings, such as happiness when others are kind or sadness and pain when they are cruel. This recognition of similarities could result in an awareness on the part of the nonhandicapped students that students with severe handicaps are hurt when they are ridiculed, laughed at, locked away from other members of the community, feared, ignored, or denied opportunities to do many of the things nonhandicapped people are allowed to do. It also could result in an awareness that many students with severe handicaps experience feelings of warmth, happiness, and joy when accepted and respected by others.

Understanding Differences

As previously noted, differences of students with severe handicaps are usually readily recognized by nonhandicapped students. While the pronounced physical, intellectual, and/or emotional differences of many students with severe handicaps are recognized, most nonhandicapped students have not been provided the information and guided experiences necessary to understand and thus feel comfortable with individuals who display such differences. Differences that are of concern, and are meaningful and understandable to nonhandicapped students, involve the functional differences in the abilities of a peer. These include such abilities as the severely handicapped student's ability to walk, learn, turn a jump rope, communicate, and handle a stressful playground situation. Differences frequently addressed that often are not meaningful to young nonhandicapped students include such areas as syndromes, genetic defects, and incidence of a handicapping condition. Such nonfunctional information is often not useful in the day-to-day interactions with individuals who experience handicaps and may even be confusing to the nonhandicapped student in regard to how he or she is supposed to use this information when interacting with a peer who experiences a severe handicap.

In teaching students about individual differences, one approach is to consider differences in abilities in regard to all individuals, including mild differences of their own and their classmates. This is generally a useful way to clarify the concept that everyone is different and to help nonhandicapped students relate to and understand the more pronounced differences of some students with severe handicaps.

Dealing with Differences

Once recognition and understanding of individual differences in abilities among students with severe handicaps is achieved, the next step is to teach nonhandicapped students how to best determine flexible approaches and ways to help their fellow students circumvent differences that may interfere with a desired activity. For example, if a group of girls want to play jump rope, a blind, uncoordinated child with an intellectual delay may be given a partner who holds her hand, tells her when to jump, and jumps with her in order to allow her to play with everyone else.

Physical Differences

The easiest and most concrete information to present when teaching nonhandicapped students to deal with differences is in the area of physical differences. Learning how to make environmental modifications to accomodate for physical disabilities, generally speaking, requires very concrete, visible adaptations in the environment to enable an individual with a severe handicap to participate in an activity. For example, in the classroom, desks may need to be pushed further apart so a wheelchair can be pushed through or a table may need to be raised so a child's wheelchair can easily slide under it. Such modifications present concrete problem-solving activities that offer a high probability of the nonhandicapped students meeting the challenge successfully.

Intellectual and Emotional Differences

Once the skill of adapting the environment to meet physical differences is mastered, nonhandicapped students can be taught to make the necessary adaptations for variances in intellectual abilities by, for example, modifying and simplifying rules and materials and learning to use the basic teaching-guiding techniques of cueing, modeling, and prompting. Adaptations for emotional or behavioral differences, often considered the most complex and abstract, may require nonhandicapped (and handicapped) students to develop appropriate reactions to desirable and undesirable behavior. These skills can assist students in recognizing and appropriately dealing with the influence of environmental factors on a variety of behaviors.

Activities for Teaching about Human Differences

A few examples of activities that classroom teachers could employ to foster understanding and respect for human differences are outlined in this section. Teachers can assist their students in learning about human differences in many ways. These can include such activities as role playing, films, discussions, and having handicapped guest speakers. For example, students can role-play a difference they have noticed in some children and/or experience a handicapping condition for a day. A child may be blindfolded to simulate blindness. Another child may *not* be allowed to talk and be required to figure out how to communicate without voice or hands. Still another child may be confined to a wheelchair for a day. Along with informative films, film with no sound or garbled sound can be used and the children can be required to explain and/or answer questions about the film's content. Discussions in groups where individual students explain their own differences and describe how others react to them and how they deal with these reactions is a good activity. Objectivity and positiveness about human differences must be stressed since group discussions that develop into pity sessions and/or negative stereotyping sessions can interfere with the development of accepting attitudes. The reader is referred to Chapter 13 for additional information regarding activities for teaching about human differences.

Human differences training can be included as an integral part of various subject areas rather than as an isolated component. Supplemental reading assignments for reading practice can be selected regarding some aspect of human differences, language arts can include an assignment to learn and practice sign language, and social studies can evaluate jobs in the community that can be done by individuals with various handicaps. The inclusion of these activities and projects into various curricular areas should begin early for all students, before barriers to human differences due to lack of understanding develop.

GUIDED EXPERIENCES

Along with the daily interaction experiences that nonhandicapped students normally have with handicapped students on the bus, in the lunchroom, and on the playground, nonhandicapped students should be provided guided, structured experiences with students with severe handicaps. These guided experiences are needed to bridge the gap between the cognitive knowledge gained in the classroom setting and the ability to use the information on a daily basis. Guided experiences should be carefully structured by the teacher to reinforce the concepts or objectives being focused on in classroom training.

Such experiences can be provided by joining a nonhandicapped class and a class for students with severe handicaps during designated periods several times a week. The time and activity emphasized should be determined jointly by regular and special class teachers. See Chapter 3 for examples of the types of activities that many students with severe handicaps and nonhandicapped students can successfully participate in together. According to Johnson, Rynders, Johnson, Schmidt, and Haider (1979), the level of sophistication of the particular contribution required of each student for any activity chosen should be individualized according to his or her unique abilities; all of the students should be encouraged to help each other.

Making a picture collage about summer vacations, brothers and sisters, or pets from family album pictures brought by each child may be a project that both handicapped and nonhandicapped children can share. When working jointly with students who experience severe handicaps on projects such as the one discussed here, nonhandicapped children are given the opportunity to strengthen the concepts learned in classroom training. For example, the collage activity could be used to reinforce the concepts of similarities among individuals; that is, students with severe handicaps are like everyone else—they have families, pets, favorite activities, and feelings.

It should be noted that teachers, when organizing guided experiences, should use techniques and methods found to be effective in fostering positive interaction experiences between students with handicaps and nonhandicapped students. For example, the use of small integrated group structures and cooperative learning tasks (Johnson & Johnson, 1980) should help enhance the probability of successful positive interactions among students with severe handicaps and nonhandicapped students. The reader is referred to Chapter 5 for more detailed information regarding procedures for promoting interactions between students with severe handicaps and nonhandicapped students.

Such experiences, along with the general interaction experiences occurring on a daily basis in the lunchroom, on the bus, and on the playground will provide a strong base from which nonhandicapped students can assimilate, on an operational level, the concepts being learned in the classroom.

CONCLUSION

Once nonhandicapped students have reached the level of effectively interacting with their handicapped peers, they should be taught how to teach other untrained, uninformed nonhandicapped individuals about individuals with severe handicaps. In addition, the nonhandicapped students should be guided in the development of the necessary skills and of an attitude of responsibility in advocating for persons experiencing severe handicaps. When we, as educators, have reached the stage of training nonhandicapped students to advocate for the needs of handicapped students, we will have built safeguards into our educational structure for perpetuating opportunities for the normalization of community living for handicapped citizens. As Donaldson (1980) stated:

> Until disabled persons are seen as individuals who, like all people, have differing skills, interests, and personality traits, the ultimate outcome of legislation mandating integration and equal opportunity will

be unpredictable—handicapped persons will continue to bear the consequences of unfavorable expectations and fear on the part of persons who control their life opportunities. (p. 504)

Finally, it should be noted that as the integration movement progresses and becomes more of a reality throughout the nation there will be increasing opportunities for all young nonhandicapped persons to learn firsthand throughout their school years about individuals with severe handicaps. As a result, the need for the education of nonhandicapped students in regard to persons with severe handicaps will become less of a burden in the future. As noted by Brown et al (1979), when students with severe handicaps and nonhandicapped students attend the same schools from childhood onward, the chances of nonhandicapped persons learning tolerance, understanding, and acceptance of differences are enhanced substantially. In other words, in integrated school settings, many young nonhandicapped persons will be given opportunities daily to learn ways to interact naturally with and understand individuals who experience severe difficulties in physical, emotional, and/or learning characteristics. The benefits of such integration will ultimately be felt by the community at large, for it is the young nonhandicapped students of today who will tomorrow be the parents, teachers, therapists, lawyers, and neighbors of handicapped individuals.

REFERENCES

Brown, L., Branston, M., McClean, M. B., Baumgart, D., Vincent, L., Falvey, M., & Schroeder, J. (1979). Using the characteristics of current and subsequent least restrictive environments in the development of curricular content for severely handicapped students. *AAESPH Review, 4*, 407-424.

Burton, T., & Hirshoren, A. (1979). The education of severely and profoundly retarded children: Are we sacrificing the child to the concept? *Exceptional Children, 45*, 598-602.

Cummings, M. (1974). *Individual differences: An experience in human relations for children.* Madison, WIS: Madison Public Schools.

Donaldson, J. (1980). Changing attitudes toward handicapped persons: A review and analysis of research. *Exceptional Children, 46*, 504-514.

Johnson, D., & Johnson, R. (1980). Integrating handicapped students into the mainstream. *Exceptional Children, 47*, 90-98.

Johnson, R., Rynders, J., Johnson, D., Schmidt, B., & Haider, S. (1979). Producing positive interaction between handicapped and non-handicapped teenagers through cooperative goal structuring: Implications for mainstreaming. *American Educational Research Journal, 16*, 161-168.

Stainback, S., & Stainback, W. (1982). Non-handicapped students' perceptions of severely handicapped students. *Education and Training of The Mentally Retarded, 17*, 177-182.

Voeltz, L. M. (1980). Children's attitudes toward handicapped peers. *American Journal of Mental Deficiency, 84*, 455-464.

Section IV

Educating Students with Severe Handicaps

Chapter 9

Assessing and Teaching Social Interaction Skills

**Luanna H. Meyer, Ralph J. McQuarter,
and Gloria Shizue Kishi**

A crucial outcome of special education has been to increase skills in each of the various curricular domains, for example, language, motor, and self-help. Thus, special educators have focused their efforts upon teaching and documenting mastery of developmental sequences of behaviors in each of these separate curricular domains. Life, on the other hand, is not organized into these separate curricular domains, and requires the integration of the various "isolated" behaviors into functional sequences and clusters; the behaviors are part of a natural activity set which includes motor, language, social, and other skills occurring simultaneously and/or in rapid succession. In recent years, several new curricular packages have emphasized teaching behaviors in functional sequences in a natural, integrated manner. Two examples are the Individualized Curriculum Sequencing model, emphasizing instruction in sequences of interrelated behaviors (Guess & Helmstetter, in press) and Project IMPACT, emphasizing the design of educational activities which teach necessary routines in daily living in an integrated manner (Neel et al., 1983). Both of these curriculum models are based on teaching task-related behaviors that occur in criterion environments, that is, natural environments in which students currently function or will likely be functioning in the future (Brown, Nietupski, & Hamre-Nietupski, 1976).

Note: Preparation of portions of this chapter was supported in part by Contract No. 300-82-0363 awarded to the University of Minnesota from the Division of Innovation and Development, Special Education Programs, U.S. Department of Education. The opinions expressed herein do not necessarily reflect the position or policy of the U.S. Department of Education, and no official endorsement should be inferred.

However, an additional component is lacking: With rare exception, activities in the natural environment involve interactions (or the deliberate inhibition of interactions) with other persons. We need to develop social competence in persons experiencing handicaps in a manner that will prepare them to interact appropriately with other persons as they carry out specific tasks in natural environments. To do this, the specific tasks we teach persons with severe handicaps must be integrated with instruction in the social skills components needed for the performance of those tasks in natural, criterion situations with other persons. We also need to prepare nonhandicapped persons to become part of congruent (i.e., supportive) environments (Thurman, 1977).

In order to prepare students with severe handicaps as well as nonhandicapped students in the manner described above, they must be provided with opportunities to interact together throughout their school years. Such interactions are crucial to the development of the skills needed for interdependent support networks. And such interactions are crucial for quality of life. Just as few of us would deny the value of knowing how to perform task-related skills involved in living and working in the community, few of us would choose to do these things in social isolation from other persons. By incorporating social interactions into educational planning for children experiencing handicaps, we are not only preparing them to function in natural environments with nonhandicapped persons, but are also creating a context for friendships to develop and maintain over time.

This chapter includes procedures for planning, implementing, and evaluating the effects of instruction intended to develop social competence in learners with severe handicaps. Goals are *not* focused upon the assessment and teaching of isolated target behaviors—out of context—in traditional curricular domains. Instead, the procedures require that the instructional team, including the parents, begin by identifying the priority activities which seem best related to progress across the years toward maximum participation in current and future environments. Once an activity has been described through observation of nonhandicapped persons engaging in that activity, the child's discrepancies are evaluated in relationship to the performance required for full participation in the activity. Training decisions are then made based upon the child's present performance level, adaptation and prosthetic equipment needs, etc., and evaluation procedures are implemented which allow the teacher to document progress as well as to problem-solve whenever the learner is not making sufficient progress in mastering the instructional objectives. These procedures have been articulated by Brown and his colleagues and students in a series of strategy papers (Brown et al., 1979) and apply to instruction in any activity goal area.

What we have added to this model is the incorporation of the social interactions among persons engaging in those activities, with particular emphasis upon specifying the social skills which the handicapped learner must display in these interactions. Our sequence of skills required for participation in an activity will include both social and nonsocial (e.g., language, motor, etc.) behaviors, but our discussion is focused upon the social interaction skills themselves. These are the links between the various component skills in the more traditional domains, and how well they are performed has a great deal to do with whether or not the person with a severe handicap will be judged to be competent in any activity by peers (McFall, 1982).

PROCEDURES

Step 1: Select and document the value of the instructional goal or activity

The teacher should observe nonhandicapped students in natural home, work, community, and leisure situations in order to select the most appropriate social goals or activities. The teacher will want to concentrate on facilitating those social behaviors that take place as part of naturally occurring activities in integrated situations.

The *Activity Selection Checklist* (see Figure 1) allows the teacher to make decisions as to whether or not particular activities are appropriate social priority goals for students with handicaps.

Each of the items on the measure represents a program standard which has been offered in discussions of educational best practices (see, for example, Ford et al., 1984; Wuerch & Voeltz, 1982); many of them have been mandated by legislation and litigation. By acquiring the skills to engage in an activity which scores high on the *Activity Selection Checklist*, the learner will be mastering component skills that will apply to other activities in other environments. Using the checklist, we have identified peer play with the "Magical Music Stick" (flute) as an appropriate educational activity for Sara, an 8-year-old girl labeled as severely multiply handicapped. The teacher was able to identify this play interaction as preferable to another choice which had been suggested by a team member as an activity which had been successful with other students in need of leisure time-skills. As can be seen from the rating on the checklist, the more typical leisure activity of puzzle assembly (with a non-interlocking, four-piece adapted puzzle) fared poorly as a goal in comparison to the one selected.

Step 2: Conduct a nonhandicapped-person inventory for the activity

The next step is to describe the sequence of behavior needed in order to participate in the activity. This should not be done by listing what the teacher *thinks* is involved. Instead, the teacher should watch what

FIGURE 1
Activity Selection Checklist

Normalization: A concern for selecting activities that have social validity and will facilitate normalized domestic living, leisure, vocational and community integration, as well as provide opportunities for movement toward increasingly complex interactions.

	Peer play with Magical Musical Stick	Solitary play with puzzle
1. **Age-appropriateness.** Is the activity something a nonhandicapped peer would do and/or enjoy?	(Yes)/No	Yes/(No)
2. **Integration.** Does the activity occur in criterion environments which include the presence and involvement of nonhandicapped persons?	(Yes)/No	Yes/(No)
3. **Acceptability/attractability.** Is the activity considered acceptable/desirable by nonhandicapped persons who are likely to be present in the specific environment?	(Yes)/No	Yes/(No)
4. **Flexibility.** Can the activity be accessed by the individual alone as well as in a group?	(Yes)/No	(Yes)/No
5. **Degree of supervision.** Can the activity be used with little to no caregiver supervision without major modifications?	(Yes)/No	(Yes)/No
6. **Longitudinal application.** Is use of the activity appropriate across the lifespan, particularly for the adolescent and adult?	(Yes)/No	Yes/(No)
7. **Caregiver preferences.** Is the activity valued by caregivers?	(Yes)/No	Yes/(No)
8. **Multiple applications.** Is the activity useful for a variety of current and/or future environments (including seasonal considerations)?	(Yes)/No	Yes/(No)
Normalization Area of Concern Score:	$\frac{8}{8}$	$\frac{3}{8}$

Continued on next page

FIGURE 1 *Continued*

Individualization: Concern related to meeting the unique needs and interest of the individual learner.

	Peer play with Magical Musical Stick	Solitary play with puzzle
1. **Skill level flexibility.** Can the activity accommodate low-to-high entry skill levels without major modifications?	Yes/(No)	Yes/(No)
2. **Participation access.** Can the activity be accessed independently or through minimal use of partial participation, preferably involving persons available in the natural environments?	(Yes)/No	(Yes)/No
3. **Prosthetic capabilities.** Can the activity be adapted to varying handicapping conditions (sensory, motor, behavior) through normalized means?	(Yes)/No	(Yes)/No
4. **Learner preferences.** Is the activity something of interest to the learner that she or he would enjoy doing or be willing to do in order to access other benefits?	(Yes)/No	Yes/(No)
5. **Skill level development.** Does the activity provide an opportunity to develop one or more critical skills?	(Yes)/No	Yes/(No)
6. **Personal development.** Will the activity enhance personal development (e.g., physical benefits)?	(Yes)/No	Yes/(No)
Individualization Area of Concern Score:	6 / 6	3 / 6

Environmental: Concerns related to logistical and physical components of activities in current and future environments.

	Peer play with Magical Musical Stick	Solitary play with puzzle
1. **Availability.** Is the activity likely to be available, both now and in the future, in the environments the learner can access?	(Yes)/No	(Yes)/No
2. **Longevity.** Is the activity likely to remain available for a reasonable period of time (e.g., for materials: likely to last without need for major repair or parts replacement for at least a year)?	(Yes)/No	(Yes)/No
3. **Safety.** Is the activity safe, within normalized "risk-taking" limits (e.g., would not pose a serious/unacceptable risk for the learner and others in the environment)?	(Yes)/No	(Yes)/No
4. **Noxiousness.** Is the activity not likely to be overly noxious (noisy, space consuming, distracting) to others in the learner's environment?	Yes/(No)	(Yes)/No
5. **Expense.** Can the activity be accessed at reasonable cost (e.g., materials are priced reasonably or have multiple uses, transportation costs reasonable, etc.)?	(Yes)/No	(Yes)/No
6. **Minimal inference.** Can the activity be programmed effectively for performance in criterion environments through available/feasible instructional opportunities?	(Yes)/No	(Yes)/No
7. **Support/willingness.** Will persons in the environment provide opportunities for the individual to engage in the activity?	(Yes)/No	(Yes)/No
Environment Area of Concern Score:	$\frac{6}{7}$	$\frac{7}{7}$
Total Score (number of items circled "yes")	$\frac{20}{21}$	$\frac{13}{21}$

children actually do in such a situation, and list each of the component behaviors which occur during the activity in the order in which they take place (Brown et al., 1979).

It is important to remember that if the goal is social interaction, the nonhandicapped-person-inventory procedure must include the observation of peer play with the materials, not simply the observation of what one child does while playing alone. The materials themselves represent stimuli which are important in prompting and reinforcing the behaviors of the children, but the teacher also needs to determine the natural *interaction* cues, correction procedures, and consequences which will occur between two children. There are consistent responses given by each partner (such as "takes material if partner takes too long with her turn," "leaves interaction when bored," etc.) based upon the success of the interaction. How Sara reacts to these interactional cues and correction procedures is as important to the success of her experiences with peers as how well she can actually manipulate the play materials.

Teachers and related professionals are accustomed to assessing the component skills of an activity in such areas as motor and language but have generally not been provided the same kind of explicit guidelines in analyzing—for instructional purposes—the social interaction components of an activity. Table 1 provides a listing of the 11 critical components of social competence which have been included in the *Assessment of Social Competence (ASC)* developed by the Minnesota Consortium Institute for the Education of Severely Handicapped Learners (Meyer, et al., 1983). The teacher should review these functions, and, while conducting the nonhandicapped-person inventory, note opportunities (and requirements!) that the learner exhibit one or more of the various social competence functions in the interaction situation. The *ASC* should enable the teacher to determine the child's level on each function, and to work systematically toward higher levels of social competence. For example, a child with a handicap may be quite successful in *Asking for Help* through having a tantrum in order to obtain something which she or he wants. But the child's opportunities to access community environments and activities will be much improved by learning to ask for help in increasingly complex and more socially acceptable ways, varied for different situations.

Table 2 illustrates the nonhandicapped-person inventory which might be observed for our example. Note that the sequence includes motor and language skills, as well as efforts to *Initiate* (function 1 on the ASC), *Reinforce Others* (function 4 on the ASC), and *Indicate Preference* (function 9 on the ASC) which themselves involve both social and nonsocial (e.g., motor) behaviors.

Step 3: Conduct a discrepancy analysis

Sara must now be assessed on each of the steps listed for the activity. As is illustrated in Table 2, Sara can already perform steps 4, 6, and 8 (as indicated by a "+" in column 2), but not steps 1, 2, 3, 5, 7, and 10.

She could exhibit the behavior in step 9, but not in a peer situation; i.e., she would appropriately indicate that she wanted to play for the teacher, but did not use this skill in a peer interaction situation. Thus, while one perspective would refer to this as a generalization failure, the important point is that Sara does not have this step in the skill sequence until the skill occurs with a peer as well as with a teacher. The *discrepancy analysis* (Brown, Branston, et al., 1979) comparing Sara's present performance with that of a peer's on each step provides the basis for the training decisions which follow.

Step 4: Make training decisions—Content

Table 2 also lists the teacher's training decisions regarding each individual step in the activity sequence; i.e., whether or not instruction will occur on that step and, if so, any adaptations required. Sara has already mastered certain steps, which thus do not require any instruction. We recommend continued monitoring of those steps throughout the training program in order to ensure that they are maintained as new skills are acquired. For those steps that Sara cannot now perform, however, three options are possible: (a) train the behavior as described; (b) train an adaptation of that behavior—including the use of a prosthesis if needed—whenever an alternative form is needed for that individual learner; or (c) use partial participation, in which training may occur at some future time but is postponed for now.

Since the nonhandicapped-person inventory describes each step in the way it would be performed by a typical peer under natural conditions, whenever it is possible to train a new skill "as is," this would be the preferred strategy. In Sara's case, only two steps are determined to be in this category: steps 3 (pointing to her choice) and 10 (displaying the social interaction by waving "bye" to the peer). For a child with multiple disabilities such as motor impairments, sensory impairments, etc., there will be many instances in which alternative *forms* must be identified and taught in order to teach the same *function* accomplished by that step in the inventory (White, 1980). Since Sara has a severe motor disability, several of the steps in this activity are not feasible as training objectives without an adaptation. Whenever alternative forms are specified, however, the teacher should attempt to select a "least dependent" alternative (Williams & York, 1977) from among the possible adaptations and uses of prosthestics. Wuerch and Voeltz (1982) provide numerous suggestions of how to adapt leisure materials using aids which are readily available in most households

TABLE 1

The Assessment of Social Competence (ASC): A Scale of Social Competence Functions

Major Skill Needs	Definition	Sample Items	
		Level I	Level IV
1. Initiate/Gain entry	Gaining access to interaction, either to initiate an interaction or enter one already underway; begin an event/exchange.	Occasionally moves self toward another person.	Notices obvious interest in activity or item by another person, and offers participation.
2. Self-regulation	Responding in absence of specific external controlling stimuli or reinforcement (on basis of internal cues and prompts), including the inhibition of responses (self-control) in certain situations.	Shows an increase in aggressive, noncompliant and/or self-injurious behaviors when sick, injured, too hot, etc.	Will go to another room, wait for privacy, etc., before masturbating.
3. Follow rules/Routines	Adhere to minimal "rules" of activity or context; generally involves serial order routines and/or branching to alternative series.	Displays predictable sleep-wake cycle.	Follows street sign instructions, e.g., "Walk/Don't Walk" lights at intersection.
4. Reinforce others/Display affection	Providing others with positive feedback rewarding to them.	Child smiles, laughs inconsistently in response to social and/or nonsocial stimuli.	Thanks people appropriately when a service has been provided.
5. Consequate others/Punish/Extinguish	Providing others with feedback to indicate that their behavior was inappropriate, unpleasant, etc. (intent is to extinguish or reduce that behavior).	Frowns, cries, etc., inconsistently in response to social and/or nonsocial stimuli.	Protests when parent puts on coat to leave.

6. Attend to relevant situation cues	Attaining specific information needed to carry out a task or solve a problem.	Turns head in direction of sound source.	Looks for signs on bathrooms (Men, Ladies, etc.) and responds appropriately.
7. Provide information/ Describe	Verbal (vocal/nonvocal) and/or gestural behavior which shares information, feelings, etc. with others.	Shifts position in seat or bus to allow another person access to a seat.	Hands parent an oven glove when parent is trying to remove a hot item from the oven.
8. Offer/Request/Accept assistance	Providing assistance or instruction to another person, asking for help when needed, accepting help from another when it is offered.	"Fusses," cries, etc., to indicate discomfort, after a predictable amount of time in one position, and will quiet if position is changed.	Uses several words or signs which he or she uses spontaneously and reliably to request those items and events from a caregiver.
9. Indicate preference	Making a choice/decision from among alternatives available or presented by others.	Consistently looks at certain objects for a longer time than others.	When offered a choice between two types of sandwiches, selects known preferences.
10. Cope with negatives	Exhibiting alternative strategy to complete task or seek alternative interaction/activity when previous effort resulted in a negative consequence and/or difficulty in effecting needs or intent.	Becomes irritable, cries, tantrums when shopping in grocery store.	When told by teacher that answer is incorrect, will "guess" next response without thinking.
11. Leave-take/Exit	Withdrawing from or terminating an interaction, ceasing participation in an activity as desired, appropriate, etc.	Suddenly walks away in the middle of a story being read by caregiver.	Tells teacher "I'm done" when work is completed.

TABLE 2
Nonhandicapped Person Inventory, Discrepancy Analysis,
and Training Decisions

Skill Sequence	Sara's Performance	Training Decision
1. Approach others by moving to peer/s [Function: Initiate/gain entry]	Looks at peer/s, but does not approach; can push own wheelchair short distances	Adapt: Train Sara to move her wheelchair to group
2. Smiles, eye contact with peer (at least once at initiation of play) [Function: Reinforce others/display affection]	Watches others, some eye contact, rarely smiles at others	Partial participation: Alert peer/s to reinforce occurrences of eye contact and/or smiles by smiling and saying nice things
3. Points to flute (or_____) when asked by peer to select toy [Function: Indicate preference]	No response if presented with a choice of two or more toys	Train skill
4. Tolerates physical assistance to reach toy [Function: Cope with negatives]	+	(Continue monitoring)
5. Presses keys to activate flute [Function: Nonsocial motor behavior]	Has difficulty keeping flute stable; inconsistent	Adapt: Tape flute onto board and monitor performance
6. Attends to turn with flute [Function: Attend to relevant situation cues]	+	(Continue monitoring)
7. Relinquishes turn with flute to peer [Function: Follow rules/routines]	Continues to play with flute when "turn" should be over	Partial participation: peer instructed to terminate Sara's turn by signing "Want to play" and removing toy from her
8. Attends to flute play by peer [Function: Attend to relevant situation cues]	+	(Continue monitoring)
9. Says "I want to play" for turn [Function: Offer/ request accept assistance]	Signs "Want to play" for teacher, but not for peer/s	Adapt: Train sign in new interaction context
10. Waves "bye" when peer leaves [Function: Leave-take/exit]	Does not acknowledge that others are leaving	Train skill

or in the neighborhood shopping center rather than purchasing highly specialized (and thus more inaccessible in the long run) adaptations for learners with severe handicaps. Thus, in step 5, Sara's flute can easily be stabilized with tape or a moist towel. Steps 1 and 9 will, on the other hand, require the use of a wheelchair for mobility and signing in place of vocalizations. By preparing nonhandicapped peers for these alternative forms, Sara's access to other situations would also be enhanced.

Other questions, which the teacher might ask in deciding which adaptations to make, might be: Has this adaptation resulted in previous success with this learner on similar behaviors? Is it an adaptation the student can also use in other activities presenting similar difficulties? Can the adaptation be readily removed or faded at some future time or, if not, can persons in the community be trained to respond to the adapted form? Finally, will the adaptation be considered socially unacceptable or undesirable by nonhandicapped persons in the environments in which the teacher anticipates it would be used? This last question applies the principle of social validity to the adaptations as well as to the activities themselves.

The principle of partial participation can be applied to any additional steps in the sequence which the teacher feels are unable to be acquired by the learner at the present time (Baumgart et al., 1982). Partial participation requires that some person in the environment in which the activity occurs will assist the student by performing a "missing step." Whenever possible, those steps should be performed by someone in the natural environment rather than by a paid professional or a caregiver (Mom or Dad), since many nonhandicapped persons could be prepared to provide levels of assistance in a nonextraordinary way, in community environments, and in various situations. In contrast, whenever steps must be performed by the teacher or the parent, the learner is restricted in access to the activity to the times and places in which caregivers are available. In the past, whenever several steps in a task analysis involved skills which the teacher judged too difficult for the student, the result was that the student either was not allowed to access the activity at all or would be able to do so only with considerable professional assistance in highly intrusive (and unnatural) forms. By using nonhandicapped peers not as peer tutors but as natural links in a social interaction chain by applying the principle of partial participation, the peer dyad can become independent of adult intrusion while being appropriately interdependent with the dyad.

It is important to reconsider partial participation steps regularly, so that if at some later date the learner seems capable of acquiring the original or an adapted form of the skill, this step would then be taught and expected from the student. In Sara's example, step 2 is described as partial participation in which the peer is encouraged to reinforce Sara for smiling and to try to elicit smiles, etc., from

Sara. Depending upon her response, this could become an instructional objective for Sara within a short period of time. The major point is that assistance should be faded out whenever possible, while leaving the natural interdependent behaviors in place, where appropriate, as part of the social interaction.

Step 4: Making training decisions—Process

Once training decisions have been made for each step, it is time to identify the *natural* cues, correction procedures, and consequences for each step and to determine the *instructional* forms of each of these which will be used (and faded) (Falvey, Brown, Lyon, Baumgart, & Schroeder, 1980). Instruction will obviously involve the use, to some extent, of artificial instructional cues and contingencies. However, the instructional plan should attempt to use natural cues and contingencies alone or paired with instructional ones. Otherwise, the behaviors which the student acquires will occur only in the presence of artificial conditions. Many of these natural cues, correction procedures and consequences will be present in the peer interaction itself; in fact, peers can be highly effective behavior "shapers" in integrated community environments! Rather than attempting to structure instructional assistance which the teacher would provide, these peer-typical contingencies should be identified and the learner taught to respond to their occurrence. In turn, peers can be reassured that they should not "make excuses" for Sara, but may even need to be a bit more emphatic with her in asking for a turn, etc., if she does not respond to their first efforts. Table 3 lists the various natural conditions which the teacher can use in "instructing" Sara and her peers on the activity.

Step 5: Evaluate instruction

Evaluation of an intervention must answer three questions (Voeltz & Evans, 1983): 1. Has instruction resulted in a change in behavior? 2. Did the instruction take place as intended? 3. Is the resultant behavior change meaningful?

Figure 2 presents a sample data sheet to monitor the acquisition of the skills and behaviors in the interaction activity (our first evaluation question). Each step in the activity chain is recorded separately, in sequence, and "trial" data on the pupil's performance would be recorded on a probe basis. Rather than collecting continuous data, the teacher should schedule these periodic probes which, if collected according to a predetermined "random" schedule, should provide a valid picture of how the student is doing. And realistically speaking, by not collecting continuous performance data, natural interactions can

occur often without the possible intrusion of a teacher observing the children and marking down what they are doing. The *Skill Cluster Acquisition Instructional Opportunities Record* (see Figure 2) includes the recording of correct and incorrect performance, but also requires more precise information on what actually occurs on each step through use of the "Levels of Assistance Key." Just as you would individualize the form of each step for the learner, these prompting procedures should address the needs of each child.

The teacher should calculate the percentage correct every 2 weeks for the individual behavior steps (rows) and for the entire skill cluster (columns); he or she can also illustrate Sara's overall performance by circling the number in each column to graph the total number of steps done correctly that day.

This data sheet can also be used to begin to answer the second evaluation question. Very often, skills are not being learned for the simple reason that learning opportunities don't occur often enough. While the teacher does not need to record continuous trial-by-trial data on each step in the activity each day, she or he should fill in the schedule of planned instructional opportunities in the boxes on the bottom portion of the data sheet, and place a slash through those sessions which do occur. For Sara, we can see that only approximately 45% of the planned interactions actually occurred across the 2 weeks. If Sara is not making progress, perhaps the first thing to do is increase this percentage. Another way to obtain information which might explain a lack of progress is to observe the interaction qualitatively, recording anecdotal notes regarding what each person does on each step. Figure 3 represents such a problem-solving record: the teacher should watch the two children and write down any comments. Then, while the ideas are still fresh after observing the activity, the teacher should suggest possible changes in the activity sequence itself, based upon what was seen. We recommend conducting this anecdotal record once every 2 weeks for any intervention program. The *Skill Cluster Acquisition/Instructional Opportunities Record* will tell you whether the student is acquiring the skill and whether the peer and teacher are performing the planned corrections, etc. But the *Anecdotal/Functional Analysis Observation Record* allows the teacher to record unplanned variations in the activity, and based upon any evidence that the activity looks different than originally designed, make changes in the program itself or the way it is being taught.

The third evaluation question must first be addressed *before* instruction, since there is no justification for teaching skills which are not functional for the learner and/or are not valued by anyone (including Sara herself!). Once Sara has mastered the activity, however, we should evaluate the success of our intervention one step further: Have her interaction opportunities been enhanced beyond this planned situation? You might keep a diary of Sara's different interaction experiences with

TABLE 3

Natural Cues and Correction Procedures by Steps of the Discrepancy Analysis

Steps in Sequence/ Target Skill	Natural Cues	Instructional Procedures	Natural Correction Procedures/Consequences
1. Approach others	Others present	Position Sara within 2 feet of activity table. When activity begins, prompt wheelchair to group. Increase distance to 5 feet, 10 feet, etc. as performance improves.	a) If she moves to group, she can engage in activity. b) If she fails to move to group, she cannot engage in activity.
2. Smiles and has eye contact with others	Others present. Others smiling and looking at Sara	Alert peer/s to reinforce occurrence of eye contact and/or smiles by smiling and saying nice things.	a) If Sara smiles, and has eye contact, peers reciprocate and say nice things. b) If Sara does not smile or give eye contact, peers do not reciprocate and may not ask her to play with them.
3. Points to Magical Musical Stick	Peer asks "What do you want?"	Physically assist Sara to point to musical stick when shown two toys and asked to make a choice.	a) If she points to musical stick, peer offers musical stick. b) If she points to other item, peer offers that item. c) If she makes no selection, peer can select material or repeat question.

	Skill/Behavior	Condition/Adaptation	Status	Response
4.	Tolerates physical assistance to reach toy	If she has difficulty reaching toy, peer will assist	Sara has skill. Continue to monitor.	a) If she tolerates physical assistance, she will receive toy. b) If she does not tolerate physical assistance, she will not receive toy.
5.	Presses keys to activate musical stick	Musical stick on tray or lap	Adaptation made: musical stick stabilized by taping to board.	a) If she presses keys, musical stick will make musical sounds. b) If she does not press keys, musical stick will not make sounds.
6.	Attends to own turn with musical stick	Musical stick emits sounds when keys are pressed	Sara has skill. Continue to monitor.	a) If she attends to material, she can continue to press keys and listen to sounds. b) If she does not attend, peer will take music stick away or ask "What do you want?"
7.	Relinquishes turn with musical stick to peer	Peer requests musical stick	Partial participation: Peer instructed to terminate Sara's turn by signing "want to play" and taking her toy.	a) If she relinquishes turn, peer presses keys and toy emits sound. b) If she does not relinquish turn, peer will request toy again or take toy away or end interaction.
8.	Attends to musical stick play by peer	Keys pressed by peer emits sounds from toy	Sara has skill. Continue to monitor.	a) If she attends to play by peer, peer will continue to play and maintain interaction. b) If she does not attend, peer may terminate interaction or take extended turn.
9.	Signs "want to play" for turn	Musical stick present/Peer playing with toy	Sara can sign "want to play" to teachers. Train sign in the context of an interaction with a peer.	a) If she signs "want to play," peer relinquishes turn and gives her toy. b) If she does not sign "want to play," peer will extended turn or terminate interaction.
10.	Waves "bye" when peer leaves	Peer looks at Sara and says "good-bye"	Teacher will physically assist Sara in waving "goodbye" to peer.	Peer leaves. Interaction completed.

FIGURE 2
Skill Cluster Acquisition/Instructional Opportunities
Record, with a Modified Self-graphing Procedure
(2-week samples)

Levels of Assistance Key	
/	Independent
V	Verbal Prompt
PP	Partial Physical
FP	Full Physical
X	Partial Participation

Date/time and Teacher's Initials: Probe Only

	10/3 pm LM	10/4 am RM	10/10 am RM	10/11 am LM	10/14 pm LM	% Correct on Individual Behaviors (2 week sample)
10. Waves "bye" when peer leaves.	10^V	10^V	10^{PP}	$10^/$	$.10^V$	0
9. Signs "want to play" for turn.	9^{FP}	9^{FP}	9^{PP}	9^{FP}	9^V	0
8. Attend to flute and other child's play.	8	8^V	8	8	8	80
7. Relinquishes turn to peer.	7^X	7^X	7^X	7^X	7^X	0
6. Attend to turn and maintains play.	6	6	6	6	⑥	100
5. Presses keys to activate flute.	5	5^V	⑤	⑤	5	60
4. Tolerates physical assistance to reach toy.	④	4	4	4	4	100
3. Points to flute (or___) when asked by peer to select toy.	3^{FP}	③^{FP}	3^{PP}	3^V	3^V	0
2. Smiles, eye contact with peer/s (at least once at initiation).	2^X	1	1	1	1	80
1. Approaches other/s by moving wheelchair.	1^{FP}	1^V	1^V	1	1	40
	0	0	0	0	0	

Percent of Total Skill Cluster Mastered   40   30   50   50   60

	Week of: 10/3-10/7	Week of: 10/10-10/14	% Completed	
Planned Instructional	10/4 10/5 10/7	10/10 10/11 10/13	50	A.M.
Opportunities	10/5 10/4 10/6	10/12 10/14	40	P.M.
(/ = completed)			45	

FIGURE 3
Anecdotal/Functional Analysis
Observation Record

Student _____   Date of Observation _____

By Whom: _____

.Activity	*What occurred (what Sara did, peer did, problems with materials, etc.)*	*Comments by observer*	*Summary, changes, etc. by teacher*
10. Waves "bye" when peer leaves.			
9. Signs "want to play" for turn.			
8. Attend to flute by peer.			
7. Relinquishes turn to peer.			
6. Attend to turn and maintains play.			
5. Presses keys to activate flute.			
4. Tolerates physical assistance to reach toy.			
3. When asked by peer to select toy, points to choice.			
2. Smile/eye contact with peer/s.			
1. Approach/ move wheelchair.			

peers at school, and exchange this information with Sara's parents. You could assist in expanding her opportunities by plans to include Sara's nonhandicapped friends in other activities—perhaps special events—and by talking with the relevant regular education teacher to arrange for Sara to participate in similar experiences planned for her nonhandicapped friends. The eventual outcome for Sara and for the community is that these activities be integrated: There is no other way for either Sara or her peers to learn to interact with one another and function competently in heterogeneous community environments.

SUMMARY

Obviously, if persons with severe handicaps are to experience maximum participation in integrated community environments, they must begin to acquire the component skills to be judged socially competent. At the same time, the community must be able and willing to include persons with handicaps in the activities characterizing those environments. In a very real sense, it may be misleading to view *independence* as the desired outcome of appropriate educational programming for handicapped learners. It is more realistic and also more normalized to view our task in special education as developing functional *interdependence* between the learner and society. The goal of interdependence is more realistic in that the needs of many learners with severe handicaps require longitudinal support networks rather than episodic training which can be withdrawn, leaving the handicapped person to function without such supports. Yet, interdependence is more than a realistic alternative: Society is, in fact, comprised of interdependent networks of persons with whom we live and work, and few of us could maintain that we are independent in the sense of living and working and recreating in isolation from other persons. What must now occur is preparation so that the individual with severe handicaps becomes a normalized member of such mutually rewarding interdependencies.

To date, the kinds of interdependencies we have negotiated among nonhandicapped persons on the job, at home, and in the community have not been available to most persons with handicaps. Instead, paid professional caregivers and trainers perform the "missing steps" (those which the person with a handicap cannot perform) and the learner's experiences are increasingly restricted to isolation and vertical interactions with authority figures. Brown, et al. (1976) emphasized that both one-to-one instruction and homogeneous grouping by disability is neither instructionally efficient, nor does this reflect the heterogeneous reality of society. Homogeneous groupings also preclude the development of interdependencies—similar to the ones shared by nonhandicapped persons—established according to complementary strengths and interests. In contrast, if students with handicaps were instructed in the context of various heterogeneous groups, access to the environment and meaningful opportunities for participation would expand dramatically. The intent of this chapter is to illustrate the design of instructional programming to facilitate social competence in leisure and play interaction between students with handicaps and nonhandicapped students. The model and each of the techniques described are equally applicable to the design of instruction to support the integration of persons experiencing severe handicaps into other activities (e.g., vocational) as well.

REFERENCES

Baumgart, D., Brown, L., Pumpian, I., Nisbet, J., Ford, A., Sweet, M., Messina, R., & Schroeder, J. (1982). Principle of partial participation and individualized adaptations in educational programs for severely handicapped students. *The Journal of The Association for the Severely Handicapped, 7,* 17-27.

Brown, L., Branston, M. B., Hamre-Nietupski, S., Pumpian, I., Certo, N., & Gruenewald, L. (1979). A strategy for developing chronological-age-appropriate and functional curricular content for severely handicapped adolescents. *Journal of Special Education, 13,* 81-90.

Brown, L., Nietupski, J., & Hamre-Nietupski, S. (1976). The criterion of ultimate functioning and public school services for the severely handicapped student. In M. A. Thomas (Ed.), *Hey, don't forget about me: Education's investment in the severely, profoundly, and multiply handicapped.* Reston, VA: The Council for Exceptional Children.

Falvey, M., Brown, L., Lyon, S., Baumgart, D., & Schroeder, J. (1980). Strategies for using cues and correction procedures. In W. Sailor, B. Wilcox, & L. Brown (Eds.), *Methods of instruction for severely handicapped students.* Baltimore: Paul H. Brookes.

Ford, A., Brown, L., Pumpian, I., Baumgart, D., Nisbet, J., Schroeder, J., & Loomis, R. (1984). Strategies for developing individualized recreation and leisure programs for severely handicapped students. In N. Certo, N. Haring, & R. York (Eds.), *Public school integration of severely handicapped students; Rational issues and progressive alternatives.* Baltimore: Paul H. Brookes.

Guess, D., & Helmstetter, E. (in press). Skill cluster instruction and the Individualized Curriculum Sequencing model. In R. H. Horner, L. Meyer Voeltz, & H. D. B. Fredericks (Eds.), *Education of learners with severe handicaps: Exemplary service strategies.* Baltimore: Paul H. Brookes.

McFall, R. M. (1982). A review and reformulation of the concept of social skills. *Behavioral Assessment, 4,* 1-33.

Meyer, L., Reichle, J., McQuarter, R. J., Evans, I. M., Neel, R. S., & Kishi, G. S. (1983). *The Assessment of Social Competence (ASC): A scale of social competence functions.* Minneapolis: University of Minnesota Consortium Institute for the Education of Severely Handicapped Learners.

Neel, R. S., Billingsley, F. F., McCarty, F., Symonds, D., Lambert, C., Lewis-Smith, N., & Hanashiro, R. (1983). *Teaching autistic children: A functional curriculum approach.* Seattle: University of Washington College of Education.

Thurman, S. R. (1977). The congruence of behavioral ecologies: A model for special education programming. *Journal of Special Education, 11*, 329-333.

Voeltz, L. M., & Evans, I. M. (1983). Educational validity: Procedures to evaluate outcomes in programs for severely handicapped learners. *The Journal of The Association for the Severely Handicapped, 8*, 3-15.

White, O. R. (1980). Adaptive performance objectives: Form versus function. In W. Sailor, B. Wilcox, & L. Brown (Eds.), *Methods of instruction for severely handicapped students*. Baltimore: Paul H. Brookes.

Williams, W., & York, R. (1977). *Vermont Minimum Objectives Curriculum*. Burlington: University of Vermont Center for Developmental Disabilities.

Wuerch, B. B., & Voeltz, L. M. (1982). *Longitudinal leisure skills for severely handicapped learners: The Ho'onanea curriculum component*. Baltimore: Paul H. Brookes.

Chapter 10

Using Peers in the Education of Students with Severe Handicaps

Many nonhandicapped students have expressed positive and accepting attitudes toward students with severe handicaps (McHale & Simeonsson, 1980; Voeltz, 1980, 1982). In addition, many nonhandicapped students want to learn more about students with severe handicaps and become more involved in assisting them to function in regular schools (Stainback & Stainback, 1982a). Thus, nonhandicapped students represent a readily available source of manpower in regular public school settings to assist students with severe handicaps.

The authors' purpose in this chapter is to discuss how nonhandicapped students could become more integrally involved in the education of students with severe handicaps. The chapter is divided into two sections. Included in the first section is a review of six ways nonhandicapped students could assist in the education of handicapped students. Included in the second section is a discussion of several practical issues to consider when nonhandicapped students become involved in the education of students with severe handicaps. Also considered in the second section is a potential pitfall that can develop from overemphasizing nonhandicapped peer involvement procedures; that is, the danger that some nonhandicapped students could develop charitable, pity-like attitudes and behaviors toward their peers with severe handicaps.

NONHANDICAPPED PEER INVOLVEMENT PROCEDURES

Researchers and other school personnel have explored a variety of nonhandicapped peer involvement procedures. Six procedures that have been found to be useful in the education of students with severe handicaps are discussed here. These are special friends, peer partners, peer modeling, social bids, peer reinforcement, and peer tutoring.

Special Friends

At the very simplest level, nonhandicapped students can assist in the education of students with severe handicaps by being friends. Voeltz, Johnson, and McQuarter (1983) have provided a succinct description of what is meant by "special friend."

> The emphasis is upon friendship and social/leisure time activity inter-actions. This model is based upon the assumption that handicapped and nonhandicapped children can develop meaningful social relationships (i.e., friendships) which would endure over time and extend outside of and beyond the school careers of these children. It is thus essential to the model that the children be "matched" in ways which parallel other friendship patterns, e.g., similar ages, perhaps same sex (dependent upon the ages of the children vis-a-vis "normalized" same vs. cross-sex friendships), physical accessibility to one another (living in the same neighborhood, etc.), shared interests and enjoyment of similar activities, and, of course, the children must like one another. Programs of this nature generally involve less emphasis upon information about handicapping conditions and view attitude change as an outcome of the social contact between the children. The focus instead is upon personal knowledge regarding the individual handicapped peer and how to interact with one another. Hence, the model assumes that *both* the nonhandicapped and handicapped child must acquire social, play and communication skills essential to that interaction. The nonhandicapped child would not generally be taught tutoring or management skills, though s/he may be taught the *forms* of the behavioral responses to be used by his/her handicapped peer. (pp. 44-45)

While the special friends concept is rather simple and straightforward, it is probably one of the better ways of involving nonhandicapped students in the education of students with severe handicaps, particularly if the goal is to develop normalized friendships and social interaction between the students.

Peer Partners

Many nonhandicapped students help each other with various tasks in natural, nonextraordinary ways, and teachers can foster the same type of helping relationship in regard to nonhandicapped students helping students with severe handicaps (Schutz, Williams, Iverson, & Duncan, 1984). Such help can be an important factor in successfully integrating students with severe handicaps into a variety of regular school settings. Many students with severe handicaps require individual help with a wide array of rather ordinary behaviors such as finding their way down the hallway, eating lunch in the school cafeteria, and/or playing on the playground with their peers. Teachers alone may not be able to provide all the direct assistance needed. A nonhandicapped peer partner could help by just being a friend who provides assistance when needed. However, it should be noted that teachers and other school personnel should carefully supervise peer partner programs. While nonhandicapped students should learn to help students with severe handicaps in natural situations when and where appropriate, a potential problem could arise wherein nonhandicapped students learn to provide too much help (or become overprotective) in regard to their handicapped peers.

Before closing this section, it should be *stressed* that students with severe handicaps should be encouraged to help nonhandicapped students when and wherever possible. Helping behaviors should not always occur in one direction, that is, the nonhandicapped students always helping the students with severe handicaps.

Peer Modeling

In studies by Egel, Richman, and Koegel (1981) and Lancioni (1982), elementary-age nonhandicapped students successfully assisted their handicapped peers to acquire new behaviors by modeling the desired responses. However, it should be noted that many students with severe handicaps lack adequate imitative skills (Stainback & Stainback, 1980); thus it may be necessary, prior to or when employing nonhandicapped peer modeling procedures, to teach generalized imitative skills to some students with severe handicaps.

Social Bids

In an investigation by Strain, Shores, and Timm (1977), nonhandicapped peers were prompted to make social bids toward preschool students classified as severely behaviorally disordered. More specifically, they were prompted to give toys to the students with severe handicaps and to make suggestions such as "Let's play." This nonhandicapped peer intervention strategy, which resulted in a dramatic increase in the self-initiated social interactional behaviors of the handicapped students, has been replicated and found to be effective with students classified as severely retarded (Young & Kerr, 1979) and as autistic (Ragland, Kerr, & Strain, 1978; Strain, 1983). It should be noted that if the social bids procedure is used, it should be employed in the natural context of ongoing integration activities and not in nonfunctional, specially contrived segregated situations. In fact, newly learned *self-initiated* social behaviors of autistic students have been found to generalize considerably better when they are in integrated as opposed to segregated settings (Strain, 1983).

Peer Reinforcement

Nonhandicapped students can become involved in reinforcing students with severe handicaps for appropriate behaviors. They can be instructed or influenced to do this in natural ways as part of regularly scheduled school activities.

Although limited, there is some research on how nonhandicapped students can be indirectly influenced to provide more reinforcement for correct responses in natural environments to students experiencing severe handicaps. As part of a larger study, Rynders, Johnson, Johnson, and Schmidt (1980) investigated the influence of various structured learning goals on the amount of reinforcement junior-high-age nonhandicapped students provided to students with severe handicaps. Three goal structures described in Chapters 2 and 3 of this book were investigated: (a) cooperative, (b) competitive, and (c) individualistic. The cooperative structure involved achieving a goal only if other students in the group achieved their goals. In the competitive structure, a student achieved his or her goal only if other members of the group failed to reach their goals. In the individualistic structure, goal attainment of group members was unrelated to the success of an individual.

The findings indicated that, in the cooperative structure, the non-handicapped students provided significantly more praise, encouragement, and support to their peers with severe handicaps than they did in either the competitive or individualistic goal structure. A major implication of this study is that nonhandicapped students can be influenced to provide more reinforcement to students with severe handicaps by the way group activities are structured.

Peer Tutoring

Peer tutoring has long been used as a part of regular school activities. Many nonhandicapped students often tutor each other in a variety of school and extracurricular activities. This same type of normalized tutoring should be encouraged between nonhandicapped students and students with severe handicaps (Kohl, Moses, & Stettner-Eaton, 1983).

Peer tutoring, a procedure in which one student is designated to provide prompts and consequences for the behavior desired of another student or small group of students, has been an effective method of instruction. In a study by Strain, Kerr, and Ragland (1979), a tutor was trained in the appropriate use of (a) specific prompting statements such as "Roll the ball to ..." and (b) verbal reinforcers such as "Good ..." to teach two elementary-age students labeled autistic to emit positive social play behaviors toward each other. The peer tutoring resulted in a significant acceleration of the positive social behaviors of the students with severe handicaps. Other researchers also have successfully employed peer tutors to teach new behaviors to students with severe handicaps (Lancioni, 1982; McHale, Olley, Marcus, & Simeonsson, 1981; Kohl, Moses, & Stettner-Eaton, 1984). Thus, peer tutoring appears to hold promise as a potentially beneficial procedure.

It should be noted that in activities such as peer tutoring in which the nonhandicapped student takes the role of an "instructor," it is generally helpful to assign an older nonhandicapped student to teach a younger student since this is a more normalized tutoring approach and can assist in avoiding the development of a potentially condescending attitude toward handicapped students of the same chronological age.

A caution, suggested by Hartup (1964), it should be noted here also. Hartup pointed out that in the peer tutoring process, the tutor-tutee relationship can evolve into a formal authoritarian role for the tutor in which the tutor totally dominates the tutee. Such a relationship may be counter-productive particularly in terms of socialization objectives. Thus, teachers should provide guidance and supervision in tutoring activities to avoid such potential pitfalls.

CONSIDERATIONS FOR CLASSROOM USE

Intervention strategies involving nonhandicapped peers represent one option for developing, accelerating, and/or maintaining the desirable behaviors of students experiencing severe handicaps. Some potential nonhandicapped peer involvement procedures were discussed in the previous section. The following discussion focuses on a few critical variables classroom teachers should consider when planning and/or implementing nonhandicapped peer intervention procedures.

Scheduling and Organizational Arrangements

Nonhandicapped peer intervention procedures can occur as part of typical integrated school activities. Joint student activities between nonhandicapped students and severely handicapped students such as recess, lunch, assembly programs, art, music, physical education, special school projects, and field trips can provide opportunities for nonhandicapped peers to become involved in the education of students with severe handicaps (Stainback, Stainback, & Jaben, 1981). In other words, peer intervention procedures should become an integral part of ongoing school programs and activities rather than a separate entity in isolated, nonfunctional settings.

Nonhandicapped students should never be pulled from their classes or their own studies to become involved in the education of students with severe handicaps. Just like students with severe handicaps, nonhandicapped students are in school to study and learn. They can become involved in the education of their peers with severe handicaps in the hallways, during recess, lunch, and at other times that they are naturally together.

Determining Tasks

A primary consideration in any training approach is the determination of the desirable behaviors to be fostered. Both teachers and any nonhandicapped peers functioning as tutors or "instructors" need to be able to evaluate and choose those behaviors that are age-appropriate and functional for students with severe handicaps. Age-appropriate behaviors foster the social acceptability of students with handicaps in natural environments, and functional behaviors enhance their chances of learning to live in natural community environments. Logically, if the behaviors taught through peer intervention procedures are not age-appropriate and functional, the potential benefits of nonhandicapped peer intervention will be negated.

Evaluating Student Skills

Prior to the selection and implementation of any specific peer intervention strategy, the skills of both the severely handicapped students and the nonhandicapped students should be carefully evaluated. For the nonhandicapped students, characteristics such as attitudes toward persons with severe handicaps should be considered. A nonhandicapped student who does not have a positive attitude toward students with handicaps will need additional training, guidance, and/or supervision from teachers when he or she participates in a nonhandicapped peer intervention procedure. A nonhandicapped student who lacks a positive attitude toward fellow students with severe handicaps should not be excluded automatically from peer intervention procedures, since his or her negative attitude might improve through guided contact and positive experiences with peers who experience severe handicaps (Voeltz, 1980, 1982). Conceivably, carefully structured interaction experiences could be used as one way of improving the attitudes of selected nonhandicapped students toward peers with severe handicaps (Stainback & Stainback, 1982b, 1982c). However, as noted above, nonhandicapped students who possess negative attitudes or other characteristics that could impede their ability to carry out successfully a particular intervention procedure will need additional attention from teachers in the form of training, guidance, and/or supervision.

The characteristics of the students with severe handicaps, such as imitative skills, verbal ability, and/or motoric and sensory abilities, also require consideration prior to the development or implementation of nonhandicapped peer intervention procedures. For example, if modeling is to be part of a particular nonhandicapped peer intervention strategy, imitation training may be necessary for those students with severe handicaps who lack adequate imitation skills. In short, the individual skills of both the students with severe handicaps and nonhandicapped students should be evaluated and used as a basis for the selection and/or development of nonhandicapped peer intervention procedures.

Training Nonhandicapped Students

Nonhandicapped peer involvement procedures with students who experience severe handicaps have been found to be effective more often when the nonhandicapped students were specifically trained in systematic peer involvement techniques (Kohl, Moses, & Stettner-Eaton, 1983, 1984; Schreibman, O'Neill, & Koegel, 1983; Strain & Kerr, 1981). Nonhandicapped students have been prompted to make social bids toward students with severe handicaps, apply consequences, and model behaviors for them.

Teachers should observe naturally occurring integrated situations to select the most appropriate cueing, modeling, and/or consequating behaviors to foster in nonhandicapped students. The teacher will want to foster those cueing, modeling, etc., behaviors that occur as part of natural social interaction situations. A great deal of training also can take place within the context of noncontrived integration activities. For example, during recess, the teacher could unobtrusively prompt a nonhandicapped student to make a social bid or reinforce a nonhandicapped student for positively consequating an appropriate play behavior of a peer with a severe handicap.

Determining the Impact

School personnel should evaluate the impact of peer involvement procedures on both the students experiencing severe handicaps and the nonhandicapped students involved. One major concern is whether or not the procedure is fostering the desirable behaviors that it was designed to foster. If a particular procedure is effective, school personnel should have data to document its effectiveness. If a procedure is ineffective and/or causing unwanted side effects (problems), this should be determined as early in the programming sequence as possible so that necessary modifications can be made.

It should be noted that evaluation is essential when implementing peer intervention procedures since there are potential problems. For example, some students with severe handicaps may respond infrequently to the social bids of their nonhandicapped peers, thus thwarting the enthusiasm of the nonhandicapped peers for continuing to initiate social bids. If such low responding is detected, modifications of nonhandicapped student training and/or teacher-administered reinforcement procedures may be needed to keep the nonhandicapped student(s) initiating social bids until the severely handicapped students' rate of responding is increased. In addition, some nonhandicapped students may not be particularly suited for working with students who experience severe handicaps because of poor attitude, impatience, and/or the inability to apply appropriate instructional techniques. Another problem relates to the possible development of charitable-like condescending attitudes and behaviors on the part of nonhandicapped students toward students with severe handicaps. Without continuous and systematic evaluation, such potential problem areas could go undetected.

For the students with severe handicaps, a non-handicapped peer involvement procedure used, for example, to foster social interactions may result in numerous brief isolated episodes of social responses rather than ongoing natural social interactional behavior (Strain & Kerr, 1981). Modification of procedures might be necessary to enhance the emission of more meaningful sustained interactions.

Positive Relationship Development

Finally, and perhaps most important, is the development of positive peer relationships (Voeltz, 1984). In all types and all aspects of peer relationships, it is critical that positive regard and mutual respect be developed between and among the students. Both the nonhandicapped students and the students with severe handicaps should acknowledge and respect differences in one another. In peer involvement activities we must systematically foster an awareness and willingness to assist any peer, whether labelled handicapped or not, if assistance is needed. In other words, all children should learn to be kind and helping toward each other. Obviously, this is a desirable goal. However, attitudes of authoritarianism, dependence, superiority, inferiority, pity, or nurturance among peers cannot be tolerated, if a goal of mutual respect is to be realized. This is a particularly salient pitfall in those activities and approaches in which one student is consistently being grouped into the "helper" category and another into the "to-be-helped" category, as when nonhandicapped students are involved in the education of students with severe handicaps. Thus, in developing understanding and altruistic relationships, we must seriously guard against development of any stereotypic "them-vs.-us" mentality that can lead to condescending social attitudes toward some students, in this case students with severe handicaps.

CONCLUSION

Many nonhandicapped students apparently would like to have more contact with and learn more about students who experience severe handicaps (Stainback & Stainback, 1982a). One way this could be accomplished is through the implementation of nonhandicapped student intervention procedures. Researchers have found that a nonhandicapped student can simply be a special friend to a peer with a severe handicap or can successfully prompt, administer consequences, and/or model appropriate behaviors for peers with severe handicaps. Thus, teachers of students with severe handicaps should consider working with regular class teachers to organize increased involvement of nonhandicapped students in the education of students experiencing severe handicaps.

There are potential advantages for both nonhandicapped students and students with severe handicaps. For example, nonhandicapped students could gain an increased understanding of severe handicapping conditions (McHale & Simeonsson, 1980) and more positive attitudes toward persons who experience severe handicaps (Voeltz, 1980, 1982). At the same time, students with severe handicaps could gain a variety of desirable behaviors as a result of the additional instructional attention (Egel et al., 1981; Strain & Kerr, 1981; Strain, 1983).

While there are potential benefits to be derived from nonhandicapped students becoming involved in the education of students with severe handicaps, there is little evidence that the benefits can be realized if nonhandicapped peer intervention procedures are not well planned and supervised. There are also potential pitfalls. Thus, school personnel should strive to plan and supervise nonhandicapped student intervention procedures with care to ensure that the experiences provided are positive and rewarding for everyone involved.

REFERENCES

Egel, A., Richman, G., & Koegel, R. (1981). Normal peer models and autistic children's learning. *Journal of Applied Behavior Analysis, 14*, 3-11.

Hartup, W. (1964). Friendship status and the effectiveness of peers as reinforcing agents. *Journal of Experimental Child Psychology, 1*, 1954-1962.

Kohl, F., Moses, L., & Stettner-Eaton, B. (1983). The results of teaching fifth and sixth graders to be instructional trainers with students who are severely handicapped. *The Journal of The Association for Persons with Severe Handicaps, 8*, 32-40.

Kohl, F., Moses, L., & Stettner-Eaton, B. (1984). A systematic training program for teaching non-handicapped students to be instructional trainers of severely handicapped schoolmates. In N. Certo, N. Haring, & R. York (Eds.), *Public school integration of severely handicapped students*. Baltimore: Paul Brookes.

Lancioni, G. E. (1982). Normal children as tutors to teach social responses to withdrawn mentally retarded schoolmates: Training, maintenance, and generalization. *Journal of Applied Behavior Analysis, 15*, 17-40.

McHale, S., Olley, J., Marcus, L., & Simeonsson, R. (1981). Non-handicapped peers as tutors for autistic children. *Exceptional Children, 48*, 263-265.

McHale, S. M., & Simeonsson, R. J. (1980). Effects of interaction on non-handicapped children's attitudes toward autistic children. *American Journal of Mental Deficiency, 85*, 18-24.

Ragland, E. E., Kerr, M. M., & Strain, P. S. (1978). Effects of social initiations on the behavior of withdrawn autistic children. *Behavior Modification, 2*, 265-578.

Rynders, J., Johnson, R., Johnson, D., & Schmidt, B. (1980). Producing positive interaction among Down's syndrome and non-handicapped teenagers through cooperative goal structuring. *American Journal of Mental Deficiency, 85*, 268-273.

Schreibman, L., O'Neill, R., & Koegel, R. (1983). Behavioral training for siblings of autistic children. *Journal of Applied Behavior Analysis, 16*, 129-138.

Schutz, R., Williams, W., Iverson, G., & Duncan, D. (1984). Social integration of severely handicapped students. In N. Certo, N. Haring, & R. York (Eds.), *Public school integration of severely handicapped students*. (pp. 15-42). Baltimore: Paul Brookes.

Simpson, R. (1980). Modifying the attitudes of regular class students toward the handicapped. *Focus on Exceptional Children, 13*, 1-11.

Stainback, S., & Stainback, W. (1980). *Educating children with severe maladaptive behaviors*. New York: Grune & Stratton.

Stainback, S., & Stainback, W. (1982a). Non-handicapped students' perceptions of severely handicapped students. *Education and Training of the Mentally Retarded, 17*, 177-182.

Stainback, W., & Stainback, S. (1982c). Integrating severely handicapped students into regular schools. In R. Rutherford (Ed.), *Severe behavior disorders of children and youth*. (pp. 49-59). Reston, VA: Council for Children with Behavioral Disorders.

Stainback, W., & Stainback, S. (1982b). Social interactions between autistic students and their peers. *Behavioral Disorders, 7*, 75-81.

Stainback, W., Stainback, S., & Jaben, T. (1981). Providing oppportunities for interaction between severely handicapped and non-handicapped students. *Teaching Exceptional Children, 13*, 72-75.

Strain, P. (1983) Generalization of autistic children's social behavior change: Effects of developmentally integrated and segregated settings. *Analysis and Intervention in Developmental Disabilities, 3*, 23-34.

Strain, P. S., & Kerr, M. M. (1981). Modifying children's social withdrawal: Issues in assessment and clinical intervention. In M. Hersen, R. Eisler, & P. Miller (Eds.), *Progress in behavior modification* (Vol. 2, pp. 203-2342). New York: Academic Press.

Strain, P. S., Kerr, M. M., & Ragland, E. U. (1979). Effects of peer-mediated social initiations and prompting/reinforcement procedures on social behavior of autistic children. *Journal of Autism and Developmental Disorders, 9*, 41-54.

Strain, P. S., Shores, R. E., & Timm, M. A. (1977). Effects of peer social initiations on the behavior of withdrawn preschool children. (1977). *Journal of Applied Behavior Analysis, 10*, 289-298.

Voeltz, L. (1980). Children's attitudes toward handicapped peers. *American Journal of Mental Deficiency, 84*, 455-464.

Voeltz, L. (1982). Effects of structured interactions with severely handicapped peers on children's attitudes. *American Journal of Mental Deficiency, 86*, 380-389.

Voeltz, L. (1984). Program and curricular innovations to prepare children for integration. In N. Certo, N. Haring, & R. York (Eds.). *Public school integration of severely handicapped students.* (pp. 155-183). Baltimore: Paul Brookes.

Voeltz, L., Johnson, R., & McQuarter, R. (1983). *The integration of school-aged children and youth with severe disabilities.* Minneapolis: Minnesota Consortium Institute, University of Minnesota.

Young, C., & Kerr, M. (1979). The effects of a retarded child's social initiations on the behavior of severely retarded school-aged peers. *Education and Training of the Mentally Retarded, 142*, 185-190.

Section V

Additional
Considerations

Chapter 11

Taking Full Advantage of Interaction Opportunities

Susan Hamre-Nietupski and John Nietupski

When students with handicaps are placed in regular public schools, teachers involved in successful integration experiences are often amazed at the abundance of opportunities for positive interactions which could occur every school day. Opportunities exist from the beginning of the day when students are entering the halls, interacting with each other and using lockers, throughout the day at recess, lunch, library, and special activities to the end of the day when waiting for buses or participating in extracurricular activities. Teachers who have been involved in integrating students with severe handicaps have found that, in order to take full advantage of the available interaction opportunities, careful *planning* is required. In other words, positive interactions between students experiencing severe handicaps and others in a regular school environment will rarely happen "spontaneously," but must be planned for in a systematic fashion.

In this chapter, the authors intend to present activities special and regular education teachers could use to take full advantage of the numerous interaction opportunities available for severely handicapped students attending regular public schools. The activities which will be presented here have been used successfully in several regular public school environments in which the authors have been involved. These activities have been employed successfully in small rural communities, as well as in medium and large metropolitan districts in Iowa and Wisconsin (Hamre-Nietupski & Nietupski, 1981; Hamre-Nietupski, Nietupski, Stainback, & Stainback, 1984; Neitupski, Hamre-Nietupski, Schuetz, and Ockwood, 1980). Many of the activities presented have also been documented as effective in recent research literature (see Donaldson, 1980: Stainback & Stainback, 1981; and Voeltz, 1982).

In order to ensure that positive interaction opportunities are taken advantage of, maintained, and enhanced as the school year progresses, the authors recommend that teachers use *several* of these activities in combination during the school year. Additionally, it is recommended that teachers continue to use these activities *throughout the entire school year*, not only at the beginning of the year.

The following information, then, will focus on numerous activities which could involve many people: special education teachers, regular education teachers, students with severe handicaps, nonhandicapped students, school administrators, parents of students with severe handicaps, and parents of nonhandicapped students. Both formal and informal activities which could be used either prior to the actual transition of handicapped students to a regular school, at the beginning of the school year, or any time throughout the school year are presented.

SUGGESTED ACTIVITIES

Teachers involved in integration efforts could provide information to all other staff members. Information meetings could be held prior to the beginning of the school year (e.g. in the spring and/or summer prior to the actual integration of students with severe handicaps into the regular school) and on several occasions throughout the year for all staff members who will be involved with students who experience severe handicaps. These information meetings might include administrators, staff in direct teaching roles, support staff (e.g. communication therapist, physical therapist), as well as nonteaching staff (e.g., secretaries, custodians, lunchroom personnel). Special and regular education staff should be encouraged to meet together whenever possible. An initial information meeting might include, for example, accurate information on specific handicapping conditions, the goals of integrating students with severe handicaps, and federal and state legislation related to integration. Staff members could also generate their own ideas for possible integration procedures during such initial meetings.

Teachers could continue to provide information meetings throughout the school year. When integration efforts are well underway, these meetings could cover such topics as the success of developing interactions between students with severe handicaps and their nonhandicapped peers in nonacademic and/or academic situations; systematic attempts to prepare students and staff; and changes in staff attitudes toward the integration of handicapped students in the school. It has been the authors' experience that subsequent meetings can be most effective when information is presented by teachers working with students with severe handicaps. Inservice salary or credit benefits frequently can be procured for staff members who serve as inservice presentors or participants.

Special and regular education staff members could visit each other's schools. Prior to the school year in which integration is to begin, regular education teachers could visit the special education school(s) to begin to identify the needs of students with severe handicaps and to better understand how relocation to a regular public school could better meet these students' needs. Special education teachers could visit the regular school during school hours to obtain general information about the student population, the daily schedule in operation, age-appropriate behaviors, and possible opportunities for interaction. This preliminary information could be helpful to special education teachers in preparing students with severe handicaps to become an integral part of the regular school environment. Special education teachers could also use this visit for observing the accessibility of numerous facilities such as the entrances, classroom(s), restrooms, cafeteria, gymnasium, auditorium, and library and possible modifications that would be helpful (the reader is referred to Orelove and Hanley, 1979, for a useful accessibility survey instrument of regular school facilities).

Staff members could plan in advance for maximizing access to building and program usage for students with severe handicaps. It would be most helpful for special and regular education staff members and administrators to meet, preferably prior to the actual integration of students with severe handicaps to discuss issues related to maximum building and program access. Much of the information gathered in the school visits, as discussed previously, could be used effectively during these meetings. Staff could discuss issues such as the location of the classroom (Can the special education classes be dispersed throughout the school rather than isolated in the basement or in one wing?); entrance to be used (Will the students with severe handicaps be able to use the same entrance as their nonhandicapped peers?); position of handicapped students in the lunchroom (Will they sit with nonhandicapped lunchroom partners or at several tables amongst those for nonhandicapped students?). It has been the authors' experience that many modifications in typical school routines (e.g., early lunchroom arrival or departure, entering school at a separate door, sitting at a separate lunch table), made initally to minimize possible difficulties for students with severe handicaps, either were unnecessary or soon became unnecessary. Modifications of building usage, scheduling, or program access should be minimized or avoided if at all possible.

Staff should also discuss modifications, which initially might be made for students with handicaps, which could change as the school year progresses (e.g., the students with severe handicaps may arrive at lunch 5 minutes early initially, but eventually might be expected to arrive at the regular time with their nonhandicapped lunchroom partners).

It should be stressed that all staff members should be encouraged to view the initial modifications as *temporary* and *flexible*, changing as the behavior and needs of the students change. Failure to emphasize the temporary, flexible nature of initial modifications may result in difficulty in changing at a future point during the school year. Similar meetings throughout the school year may be needed to alter the situation as necessary.

Staff members will also need to discuss issues such as how the needs of students with severe handicaps in physical education, art, music, occupational and physical therapy, and communication therapy can be met within the regular school building. Transdisciplinary input from several persons will be needed, possibly including the building principal; regular and adaptive physical education, art, music teachers; occupational therapists; physical therapists; and communication therapists as well as special and regular education staff. If regular education teacher(s) will include students with severe handicaps in their programming, other specific issues may need to be addressed, including scheduling, functional curriculum objectives, and the amount of support needed from the special education staff, for example.

Administrator could be encouraged to employ a staff member and/or consultant on a district-wide basis to work exclusively on the integration of students with severe handicaps. A designated person within the school (or school system) could work on integration activities, on a full- or part-time basis, as his or her major job responsibility. This could be a teacher or program support teacher (or similar person) whose job responsibilities are altered in order to devote time to integration efforts.

It has been the authors' experience that a staff member within the school system might be able to organize and implement the integration efforts on a day-to-day basis more effectively than a part-time consultant from outside the school district. The designated person, whether from inside or outside the system, would be responsible for planning, implementing, and evaluating efforts to integrate students with severe handicaps in one school or throughout the school system. This person could also be responsible for planning with special and regular education teachers and administrators, conducting sensitization/information sessions (disussed below) with students and staff (i.e., direct contact with students and staff members), and formally evaluating integration activities.

A school or district may choose not to assign a person solely to integration efforts. In such instances, one or more individuals at the building level should be accorded some time to coordinate integration efforts. Without such coordination, it becomes much easier to let integration efforts slide following the initial flurry of activity.

Special education teachers could locate a contact person(s) to facilitate integration activities. Many of the activities outlined in this book require considerable planning and cooperation between both special and regular education staff members and considerable time investment from all those involved. The assistance of a contact person within the regular school can bring about activities more efficiently. Schools frequently have at least one person whose responsibilities include working with other staff members in planning school- or department-wide activities. A potential contact person might be a grade or subject chairperson, a head teacher, activities coordinator, or a human relations or human services coordinator. These contact persons can be an extremely useful resource for information about scheduling for groups of staff members and students, units or topics which will be covered in various curriculum areas at different grade levels, and special upcoming school events. Contact persons can often facilitate more rapid gathering of information from or passing of information to both staff and students within a school.

Teachers could involve parents in plans to integrate students with severe handicaps. Parents of both handicapped and nonhandicapped students could be invited to participate in integration activities. Initially, preferably prior to the actual integration of students with severe handicaps into the regular school, a parent-teacher meeting could be held. Discussions could be held on the rationale for regular school placement, an outline of plans for systematic integration efforts, and provision of special and/or therapy services. Concerns of parents of both students with handicaps and nonhandicapped students also should be discussed. If parents of students with severe handicaps express concern that their children might be either physically or verbally harassed, for example, strategies for dealing with potential difficulties could be outlined at that time. Parents of students with severe handicaps should be encouraged to tour the regular school building with a staff member, preferably during school hours. Observation of the physical facility, the behavior of nonhandicapped students, and daily school activities could help provide a clearer picture of how the regular school will benefit their children. Parents should be encouraged to attend several additional school-related activities throughout the school year, including sensitization/information sessions. They should also be encouraged to become involved in a volunteer or helper capacity for school integration activities. Once integration activities are underway, presentations could be made to parents regarding both positive and negative aspects of the integration experience and alternate solutions to integration problems can be discussed. Teachers should keep parents informed of integration activities throughout the year and encourage parents to observe and participate in those activities.

In particular, parents of students with severe handicaps should be encouraged to become active members of the school's parent-teacher organization. If parents involve themselves integrally in the school program, the probability is enhanced that their children will be more integrally involved.

Teachers could request that additional school personnel (or community volunteers) be provided for support when integration is initiated. To facilitate a smooth transition of students with severe handicaps into regular school activities, staff members such as program support teachers (or other persons) could be assigned temporarily to assist in the program during the initial weeks of the semester. Areas where additional support might be needed could include getting on and off the bus; using correct entrances and exits; locating classrooms, bathrooms, offices, and other school facilities; using lockers and locks; following lunchroom procedures; and using recess time in appropriate ways.

This extra support can be of great assistance to special education teachers and to students with severe handicaps, as well as to other school staff and building principals, all of whom might feel overwhelmed by the typical "beginning-of-the-school-year hassles." It is important to plan to gradually fade out the additional support as students begin to acquire necessary skills and learn new school routines.

Staff involved in integration activities could hold a staff "drop-in" to answer questions on integration. Teachers, administrators, supervisors, program support persons, and/or other persons involved with integration activities could make themselves available for an informal "drop-in" to answer questions which both regular and special education staff members may have. Such a "drop-in" might be arranged in the semester prior to the actual integration of students with severe handicaps or early in the new school year. Informed persons should be available in the staff lounge for a period of time to allow anyone with questions or comments to stop in to discuss them. Coffee and snacks could be provided as further "encouragement" to drop in. It has been the authors' experience that staff members who may not feel comfortable asking questions or commenting about the integration of students with severe handicaps in a large staff meeting may discuss their concerns in this informal arrangement. The authors found that after "breaking the ice" with refreshments and informal conversation, teachers will ask numerous questions, express an interest in the program for students with severe handicaps, and often indicate that they are not as apprehensive as they might have been initially at the prospect of having students with severe handicaps attend the school or their class activities.

Special education teachers could join a "team" of teachers. A regular school staff is typically organized into "teams" for planning and working together. These teams are usually organized according to grade or subject matter, such as the "eighth-grade team" or the "science department." Regular and special education staff members could cooperatively organize scheduling, activities, and field trips; could exchange students, and could share resources. It is recommended that teachers include the building administration in plans to involve special education staff on a team, at least initially.

Special and regular education teachers can arrange flexible programming for individual students and team teaching arrangements. Special and regular education teachers who teach students with various handicapping conditions may observe considerable overlap in their general curriculum goals and daily programming. These teachers could arrange for integration of individual students into each other's classes for different subjects during the day to best meet each student's individual needs. Teachers might also decide that in some instances a *team teaching situation* may be extremely beneficial for their students as well as more efficient for teachers.

Special education teachers can encourage other staff members and nonhandicapped students to visit their classrooms. Initially, special education teachers can expect other staff members to display considerable curiosity about what goes on in the classroom for students with severe handicaps. Special education teachers can make other staff members feel welcome in their classrooms by announcing an "open-door-policy," a willingness to have visitors. Nonhandicapped students might also be curious about what happens in the classroom and, with appropriate permission (e.g., study hall passes, hall passes), could spend time there. Whenever appropriate, visitors could observe on-going instruction, look at the room and its materials, and interact with handicapped students. This willingness to be observed and have visitors may serve to remove some of the "mystery" that often surrounds a new classroom for students with severe handicaps which has just been located in a regular school. Eventually, this could lead to having observers, either nonhandicapped students or staff members, get involved with handicapped students.

Special education staff members should spend some of their break time in the regular staff lounge. The staff lounge provides a place for teachers to take a break from their daily teaching responsibilities. Special and regular education staff members have more opportunities to get to know one another when congregating in the lounge. The lounge provides opportunities to discuss and compare objectives, methods, activities, and community trips being planned in their classrooms. If special education staff members typically have segregated themselves in a separate lounge area, those staff members should "integrate" themselves into the regular education lounge for at least a portion of their break time. Eventually, it would be most conducive to integration to eliminate separate lounges, since it is very possible that having different lounges for special and regular education staff only serves to segregate them (and, in turn, their students) from each other.

Teachers could present sensitization/information sessions for nonhandicapped students. The authors consider this activity a key element in preparing nonhandicapped students for successful integration of students experiencing severe handicaps. The purpose of sensitization/information sessions would be to prepare nonhandicapped students to interact appropriately with their peers who have handicaps. These sessions could involve the presentation of accurate information about people experiencing handicaps and activities designed to help the participants to become more aware of and sensitive to the individual needs of all students, including those experiencing handicaps. Sessions could be presented prior to and during the actual integration of students with severe handicaps into the regular school; subsequent sessions could be presented on small (class size) and large group bases. Information could be provided by various persons including special and regular education teachers, the integration consultant, and student leaders (discussed below).

A large group session, if used, should be considered an initial lead-in to subsequent small group sessions. Large group sessions might include general information such as a brief explanation of why students experiencing severe handicaps are attending regular schools; discussion of inaccurate, stereotypic information students might have about people experiencing handicaps (the reader is referred to Budoff, Siperstein, and Connant, 1979, for a discussion of children's lack of knowledge of handicapping conditions); presentation of important accurate information about people experiencing handicaps; viewing of a movie/filmstrip about people experiencing handicaps; a question/answer period; and discussion of integration activities that could take place during the school year. It is recommended that large group sessions *not* be used as the *sole* method of providing sensitization information since large group presentations alone have not been shown to significantly modify attitudes (Forader, 1970).

Small group sensitization sessions might be held in the nonhandicapped students' regular classrooms, or the nonhandicapped students could be invited to the special education classroom (the students with severe handicaps may or may not be in the room at the time). When determining information for presentation in small group sessions, it might be possible to integrate information about handicaps into topics that are currently being worked on in regular classes. Small group sessions could include more specific information such as instructor-guided group discussion of the similarities as well as the differences among people (teachers should note that Siperstein, Bak, and Gottleib, 1977, and Donaldson, 1980, suggest that to be successful, group discussions should be based on factual information rather than opinion or emotion and with differential reinforcement provided by the instructor).

Also valuable would be discussion of the pros and cons of integrating students experiencing handicaps and simulation activities to experience temporarily what it might be like to have a disability (teachers should note that Clore and Jeffrey, 1972, and Donaldson, 1980, suggest that the most effective simulations would have the role-player be perceived as truly disabled rather than play-acting and that the role-player have the opportunity to observe the reactions of nondisabled strangers).

Other activities might include a live or videotaped presentation made by a successful disabled peer, college student, or adult (the reader is referred to Donaldson, 1980, for a discussion on the use of disabled persons as credible presentors); a movie-filmstrip about people who experience handicaps; an "assignment" to determine how the media (e.g., newspapers, magazines, television) presents people with handicaps; and viewing slides of the handicapped students who will attend the school, engaged in activities similar to as well as different from, those in which the nonhandicapped students engage. Students could be "assigned" a written paragraph in which they describe how they could make a student experiencing severe handicaps feel more a part of the school; they might also participate in a discussion of possible follow-up projects in which nonhandicapped students might participate with students experiencing severe handicaps. For more detailed information on possible sensitization/information session content, the reader is referred to Nietupski et al. (1980). The reader is also referred to Section II of this book for additional information regarding ways of educating nonhandicapped students about students with severe handicaps.

Teachers could train nonhandicapped students to serve as student leaders for sensitization/information sessions. It has been the authors' experience that nonhandicapped students can be given information about handicapped people and then, in turn, serve as student leaders in sharing similar information with their peers in sensitization/information sessions. The authors have found this to be especially useful with upper elementary age and high school students.

Initially, prospective student leaders need to be given accurate information about students with severe handicaps, information regarding the particular students attending their school, and sensitivity to the needs of people with handicaps. Student leaders could then assist in both planning and conducting sensitization/information sessions. They could help by providing their views on activities they believe their peers might find interesting and could also conduct sessions together with adult leaders. Potential student leaders could be solicited from classes or clubs such as student council, future leaders, human services, human relations, or psychology classes/programs.

Teachers could include information about people with handicaps in the regular education curriculum. If students with severe handicaps are to become truly integrated into regular schools, sensitization to handicapped peers should become an established part of ongoing curricula for nonhandicapped students. For example, sensitization/information sessions might be presented to social studies classes in a middle school during an ongoing unit on similarities and differences between people. In order to integrate information regarding people with handicaps into the regular curriculum, it would seem appropriate for special education teachers to work with regular education teachers to provide information on what to include. As another example, if sensitization/information sessions are being presented to health classes during an ongoing unit on prenatal/postnatal child care, it would seem appropriate for special education teachers to work with regular education health class teachers to make topics such as the causes and prevention of mental retardation a permanent part of the health curriculum.

It has been the authors' experience that information about people experiencing handicaps can be included in ongoing units in subjects such as in English with, for example, a discussion of the treatment of a person labeled mentally retarded in the movie Charley; in "careers" classes or "future teachers club" with teachers of handicapped students discussing, for example, why they entered the special education field and why someone might consider education of students experiencing handicaps as a profession; and human relations classes, with, for example, a discussion of how past and present treatment and rights of persons with handicaps parallels experiences of racial and ethnic minority groups.

Cooperative planning between special and regular education teachers is necessary if information on people with handicaps is going to be made a permanent part of the regular education curriculum. In most school districts this planning might also involve supervisory personnel responsible for curriculum areas on a system-wide basis. Initial efforts to build sensitization/information activities on handicaps into different subjects provides an excellent foundation for the task of eventual permanent incorporation into curricula in subsequent years.

Teachers could train nonhandicapped students to serve as tutors or partners of severely handicapped students. Recently, the use of nonhandicapped student tutors/partners to work with students experiencing handicaps has been recognized as effective (Almond, Rodgers, & Krug, 1979; Donder & Nietupski, 1981; Kohl, Moses, & Stettner-Eaton, 1984; Poorman, 1980; Stainback, Stainback, & Jaben, 1981). Initially, nonhandicapped students need to be given accurate information about their peers with severe handicaps and taught to appropriately work with them. They could then serve as tutors or partners for a variety of tasks both in the classroom (e.g. teaching individualized programs) as well as out of the classroom (e.g. using lockers, navigating hallways, eating in the lunchroom, and using recess time appropriately).

In the special education classroom, tutors can provide extra assistance to students with severe handicaps by teaching tasks designated by the classroom teacher. Tutors might work with students on self-care, communication, or functional academic tasks, for example. They could also assist students with severe handicaps in other classes such as physical education, home economics, music, or art. In one high school with which the authors have been involved, tutors worked on functional word reading tasks in the special education classroom. In a middle school setting, tutors taught roller skating in a physical education class and later accompanied their peers with handicaps to a community roller-rink.

Tutors can also be helpful in teaching outside the classroom. In a middle school in the authors' experience, nonhandicapped students who had participated in sensitization/information sessions volunteered to serve as lunchroom partners; they met their handicapped partners prior to the lunch period each day, went to the lunchroom together, sat with them during lunch, modeled age-appropriate lunchroom behaviors, and interacted with them after lunch. In still another middle school, nonhandicapped student volunteers taught game skills appropriate for the playground to their peers with handicaps (Donder & Nietupski, 1981). For additional information and some possible pitfalls to avoid in using nonhandicapped student volunteers, the reader is referred to Chapter 10 of this book.

Include students with severe handicaps in as many extracurricular activities as possible. Most schools have extracurricular activities in which students can choose to participate. Examples of such activities include clubs, sports, newspaper and yearbook staff, student council, and social events such as dances. Typically, these activities are offered after school or during lunchtime. It is very possible that students experiencing severe handicaps could acquire some of the skills necessary to participate at least partially in some of these activities. For example, in one of the middle schools in which the authors were involved, students with severe handicaps participated with their nonhandicapped peers in the production of the school newspaper by collating, stapling, and delivering the newspapers to each classroom. If at all possible, the special education classroom might elect a representative to attend student council meetings. Participation in any of these extra activities can provide students with severe handicaps and nonhandicapped students opportunities to work together in a positive manner.

Teach students with severe handicaps to participate in school jobs. Most schools have a variety of school jobs which involve relatively simple tasks such as delivering written messages, taking attendance slips to classrooms, stamping tardy passes, collating and stapling papers, stuffing envelopes in the office, and delivering/operating audiovisual (AV) equipment. These jobs are typically carried out by nonhandicapped students. It is very possible, though, that students with severe handicaps can acquire some of the skills necessary to participate at least partially in some of these school jobs. In one of the middle schools in the authors' experience, students with severe handicaps worked with nonhandicapped partners to help deliver, operate, and pick up AV equipment. Eventually, one of the students with a severe handicap was taught by her nonhandicapped partner to operate some of the AV equipment independently. York and York (1983) reported on a school in Illinois in which a multihandicapped student was taught to operate an electric wheelchair and then to collect attendance slips from all classrooms.   By assisting in school jobs, students experiencing severe handicaps can take a service-provider role rather than the usual assistance-seeker role.   Such opportunities are rarely afforded to students with severe handicaps.   Participation in school jobs has the additional advantage of providing increased visibility around the school and provides for increased interaction opportunities with nonhandicapped students and adults.

Teachers could request inservice or sensitizing nonhandicapped students to their peers experiencing handicaps.   The school administration could be asked to provide a course or workshop dealing with how to sensitize and provide information about persons with handicaps to nonhandicapped students.   Teachers who have been involved in successful integration experiences might be invited to be presenters.   It may be possible to attend a course with similar content at a university, with such courses offered by the special education and/or regular education curriculum and instruction departments.   The inservice could include information about methods of dealing with possible negative attitudes and fears of nonhandicapped students toward students with handicaps and with media that might be appropriate for providing students with accurate information about handicaps.   Inservice credit toward salary advancement might be requested as an incentive for teacher participation.   Teachers who participate could, in turn, be instrumental in leading other teachers, as well as students, in school integration activities.

Teacher could become informed of appropriate media available for sensitizing nonhandicapped students to their peers experiencing handicaps.   Both special and regular education staff members could be informed of relevant media by being involved in presentations of examples of children's books, filmstrips, and movies which might be appropriate for use with nonhandicapped students to present accurate information about people with handicaps.   Such a media presentation might be given by the school librarian in conjunction with the integration consultant and/or informed teachers. The presentation could be made at a staff meeting or inservice.   Lists of appropriate media might be provided to all teachers.   The media itself could be made available in the school instructional materials center or library for teachers as well as students to check out.   For additional information on appropriate media, the reader is referred to Chapter 13 of this book and to Nietupski et al., 1980.   For additional information on listings of appropriate media for use with elementary/middle and middle/high school students, the reader is referred to Hamre-Neitupski, 1982a and 1982b.

Teachers could encourage students to make successful integration a school "objective."   In many groups, such as student council or human relations, "objectives" or "priorities" for the school year are selected by students.   Helping to involve students with severe handicaps as an important part of the regular school could be established as an objective.   Teachers could provide students with information on several ways in which their assistance on integration efforts could be beneficial and they could then work to accomplish the necessary steps toward the objective.

Encourage nonhandicapped students to write articles for the school newspaper and/or yearbook about the integration of students experiencing severe handicaps.   Schools frequently use school newspapers and the yearbook as a means of informing all students and staff about happenings in the school. Teachers usually act as advisors for these student organizations. Students could be encouraged to write articles on integration activities involving students with severe handicaps.   The student writers could report on sensitization/information sessions and other integration activities in their articles.   In one of the middle schools in the authors' experience, nonhandicapped students "interviewed" some students with handicaps who previously had been in a self-contained school, about both the positive and negative aspects of attending a regular school. Articles also could revolve around interesting information about students experiencing handicaps and their teachers. In one elementary school, for example, students took photographs of their peers with handicaps (with appropriate parental and school approval) and wrote accompanying stories to produce their own book about students experiencing handicaps.

Teachers involved in successful integration experiences could provide information to special education teachers sending additional students with handicaps to a regular public school in the future.   If some students with severe handicaps are still placed in self-contained settings, important information concerning the types of behaviors/skills conducive to successful integration in the regular school can be provided to their teachers. Such information should *not* be provided in order to exclude any student from being integrated into a regular school; rather such information could be used in order to refine tasks and curriculum objectives currently in the self-contained setting to more accurately reflect skills which could be functional and age-appropriate in regular school settings.   This information might include, for example, age-appropriate behaviors expected in hallways, bathrooms, cafeteria, assemblies, and free time. Vehicles for distributing this information include school-system-wide newsletters or placement of information about ongoing integration activities in a centralized location, such as a staff resource materials center, for use by teachers system-wide. As an extension of this information-sharing process, teachers from the staff of a self-contained school could be invited to visit the regular school site to observe integration activities and daily school routines in operation.

SUMMARY

In this chapter, the authors have presented numerous activities which should help teachers to take greater advantage of the interaction opportunities available to students with severe handicaps in regular public schools. It is our firm conviction that the use of several of these activities in combination, on an ongoing basis, can result in the progressive inclusion of students experiencing severe handicaps into the regular public school milieu.

REFERENCES

Almond, P., Rodgers, S., & Drug, D. (1979). A model for including elementary students in the severely handicapped classroom. *Teaching Exceptional Children*, *11*, 135-139.

Budoff, M., Siperstein, G., & Conant, S. (1979). Children's knowledge of mental retardation. *Education and Training of the Mentally Retarded*, *14*(4), 277-281.

Clore, G., & Jeffrey, K. (1972). Emotional role-playing, attitude change and attraction toward a disabled person. *Journal of Personality and Social Psychology*, *23*, 105-111.

Donaldson, J. (1980). Changing attitudes toward handicapped persons: A review and analysis of research. *Exceptional Children*, *46*(7), 504-514.

Donder, D., & Nietupski, J. (1981). Non-handicapped adolescents teaching playground skills to their mentally retarded peers: Toward a less restrictive middle school environment. *Education and Training of the Mentally Retarded*, *16*(4), 270-276.

Forader, A. (1970). Modifying social attitudes toward the physically disabled through three different modes of instruction. *Dissertation Abstracts*, *30*, 4360B.

Hamre-Nietupski, S. (1982a). *Books, movies and filmstrips appropriate for sensitizing elementary/middle school students to their handicapped peers*. Unpublished manuscript, University of Northern Iowa, Department of Special Education, Cedar Falls.

Hamre-Nietupski, S. (1982b). *Books, movies and filmstrips appropriate for sensitizing middle/high school students to their handicapped peers*. Unpublished manuscript, University of Northern Iowa, Department of Special Education, Cedar Falls.

Hamre-Nietupski, S., & Nietupski, J. (1981). Integral involvement of severely handicapped students within regular public schools. *Journal of the Association for the Severely Handicapped*, *6*(2), 30-39.

Hamre-Nietupski, S., Nietupski, J., Stainback, W., & Stainback, S. (1984). Preparing a school system for longitudinal integration efforts. In N. Certo, N. Haring, & R. York (Eds.), *Public school integration of the severely handicapped: Rational issues and progressive alternatives* (pp. 107-141). Baltimore: Paul H. Brookes.

Kohl, F., Moses, L., & Stettner-Eaton, B. (1984). A systematic training program for teaching non-handicapped students to be instructional trainees of severely handicapped schoolmates. In N. Certo, N. Haring, & R. York

(Eds.), *Public school integration of severely handicapped students: Rational issues and progressive alternatives.* (pp. 185-195). Baltimore: Paul H. Brookes.

Nietupski, J., Hamre-Nietupski, S., Schuetz, G., & Ockwood, L. (Eds.). (1980). *Severely handicapped students in regular schools.* Milwaukee, WI: Milwaukee Public School.

Orelove, F., & Hanley, C. (1979). Modifying school buildings for the severely handicapped: A school accessibility survey. *AAESPH Review, 4*(3), 219-236.

Poorman, S. (1980). Mainstreaming in reverse with a special friend. *Teaching Exceptional Children, 12,* 136-142.

Siperstein, G., Bak, J., & Gottleib, J. (1977). Effects of group discussion on children's attitudes toward handicapped peers. *Journal of Educational Research, 70,* 131-134.

Stainback, W., & Stainback, S. (1981). A review of research on interactions between severely handicapped and non-handicapped students. *Journal of the Association for the Severely Handicapped, 6,* 23-29.

Stainback, W., Stainback, S., Jaben, T. (1981). Providing opportunities for interaction between severely handicapped and non-handicapped students. *Teaching Exceptional Children, 13,* 72-75.

Voeltz, L. (1982). Effects of structured interactions with severely handicapped peers on children's attitudes. *American Journal of Mental Deficiency, 86*(4), 380-390.

York, R., & York, J. (1983, October 15). Presentation at the 2nd Annual Conference of the Iowa Chapter of The Association for the Severely Handicapped, Cedar Falls, IA.

Chapter 12

Community Integration for Individuals With Severe Handicaps

Paul Wehman and Janet Hill

The integration of children and adults with severe handicaps into community activities is crucial for preventing institutionalization, enriching quality of life, and helping nonhandicapped members of society be more accepting. As the majority of the chapters in this text have indicated, educational integration is an important element of an appropriate education for individuals experiencing severe handicaps. However, it is also necessary to teach these individuals how to function in the community in a competent manner.

Community integration can occur in work settings, stores, recreation environments, and in other community locations like the post office, doctor's office, etc. Community integration skills are best taught at the actual site where the desired skill is to be performed. In this chapter we will present and discuss several steps involved in programming for community integration. First, we identify ways to select target objectives. Second, we discuss how to find community placements. Third, we list several ways to facilitate community integration. Finally, a plan for program evaluation is briefly described.

SELECTING TARGET OBJECTIVES

As the educational blueprint for the student's service needs and programmatic goals, the Individualized Education Program (IEP) is the best vehicle for administering a community integration program. Identified objectives should reflect parental needs and ability to support the program; the student's interests and present functioning level, and coordination with other objectives on the IEP.

Identifying specific instructional objectives before a community integration program is implemented avoids the pitfall of presenting isolated activities that do not meet long-range needs. The following considerations may serve as guidelines in determining target goals for program planning:

- What activities and resources are available near the student's home?
- What leisure and domestic (shopping) patterns does the student's family follow regularly, and how does the student participate in these activities?
- What social interaction strengths or deficits does the student have, and which require remediation in the community?
- What motor and/or self-care strengths or deficits does the student have, and which require remediation in the community?
- What communication strengths or deficits does the student have, and which require remediation in the community?
- What community integration activities do parents rate as a high priority (e.g., use of leisure time during shopping)?
- Based on a ranking of available community integration activities, which ones are of highest priority in terms of student need?

The functional utility of related IEP objectives will be enhanced if skills are practiced in natural community settings. For example, the student who practices use of picture communication cards in the classroom day in and day out should have the opportunity to use these cards under teacher supervision in a community setting such as a fast food restaurant. Table 1 provides some examples of community activities and settings that may be suitable for use in various curricular training areas.

Sample Goals and Objectives

Annual: John will develop at least four measurable skills to participate more fully in less restrictive community environments with friends or family. *Short-term*: Following a companion at all times, John will operate a grocery cart to 90% criterion over three consecutive trials in a neighborhood grocery store.

Annual: Sandra will exhibit appropriate social behavior in at least three community environments. *Short-term*: Sandra will comply with three directional commands (e.g., "Let's sit over here") within 10 seconds over three consecutive trials at the community recreation center.

Annual: Steve will exhibit social interaction skills with nonhandicapped persons in three different community settings. *Short-term*:

TABLE 1
Integrated Community Activities and Settings

Curricular Areas	*Activities and Settings*
Domestic Skill Training	• Real homes volunteered by school neighbors or staff • Local group homes/respite care homes • Domestic maid service office crew • Apartment/hallway clean-up crew • Home economics areas in regular schools/-universities • Nursing homes/hospital
Vocational Skill Training	• Small work crews for businesses, schools, churches, public agencies • Small grounds crews at universities, parks, churches • Volunteer agencies processing food or clothes for poor or elderly • Volunteer or paid individual job placement • Operating a concession on city streets, malls, sports events (hot dog, fruit vending, etc.)
Recreational/ Leisure Skill Training	• Mainstream students in physical education, music, art, dance classes with nonhandicapped • Involve in church groups • Use recreational facilities such as community centers, bowling, family amusement, movies, parks • Use shopping malls for shopping and window shopping
Community Functioning Skill Training	• Behavior in doctor's office/hospital • Behavior in church • Behavior on sidewalks/streets/neighborhood • Shopping for groceries, clothes, other • Behavior in restaurant/stores

Steve will greet at least five fellow Scouts by waving, smiling, or using a picture communication card during the first 10 minutes of the meeting over three consecutive meetings.

Annual: Angela will generalize functional use of picture card communication to three different community environments. *Short-term*: Without trainer assistance, Angela will order refreshments at a bowling alley snack bar over three consecutive trials.

IDENTIFYING AND SECURING PLACEMENTS

Appropriate community environments for initiating community integration activities might include: a community store, restaurant, or agency which the family regularly frequents; a club or group that nonhandicapped peers also join, such as 4-H, Scouts, or church groups; or a school activity or community recreational facility used by nonhandicapped age peers (e.g., pep rallies, a pinball arcade, Boy's Club, or community pool).

Figure 1 depicts a flow chart of steps involved in initiating and implementing a community integration placement for an individual student. To prevent a single teacher from being overwhelmed by added responsibilities, it may be useful for teachers of students of similar age groups to work together, enlisting the administrator's help as much as possible for contacts and suggestions.

Assess Community Resources.

The development of a community integration program should begin by assessing currently available community resources rather than identifying ideal community services for students with severe handicaps. This approach emphasizes integration in existing activities which are readily accessible to handicapped students and their families. Available activities may be classified according to such factors as appropriate age levels, cost variables, interest areas, and location.

Assess the Student.

Make a simple survey of what the student does during non-school hours. This information can provide an indication of how well the student and family are integrated in their community, as well as what activities they may benefit from and enjoy. Survey questions might include items such as the following:

• Does the student accompany parents on errands or appointments, to church, to visit friends, to leisure activities such as movies or bowling?
• What are the family's favorite community leisure activities?
• Do family members have time to transport the student on a weekly basis to a selected activity?

Identify Integration Needs.

Next, identify a sequence of appropriate community integration activities for the student based on availability, need, and interest. Plans for the entire school year can be developed beginning, for example, with training for appropriate social behavior and skill development in a laundromat with mother, to behavior in church by mid-year, and finally joining a neighborhood scout troop during the last quarter.

Contact Community Resources.

An initial meeting with involved persons in the community setting is a prerequisite to placement. Even if the selected environment is a commercial facility such as a grocery store, discussing the program philosophy and objectives with appropriate persons can be useful. In group settings such as clubs or troops, such a meeting will be essential, and additional orientation may be needed.

Try to observe the activity before making promises to parents or actually placing the student. Use the observation period to identify essential prerequisite skills, environmental barriers, and potential dangers. Community activities staffed by volunteers may prove unsuitable if they are loosely run. Students with handicaps and their families may be disappointed if the size of the group, ages, or activity schedules fluctuate greatly.

Conduct Orientation Programs.

Don't assume that community citizens are well informed about the nature and needs of persons experiencing severe handicaps. Most community groups or activities can benefit from a structured orientation program. Presenting visual materials is a helpful approach, such as a slide show depicting interaction between students with handicaps and nonhandicapped youths.

Facilitate Placement.

Make sure that the student arrives and leaves on time, wears appropriate clothing, and otherwise fits into the routine of the planned activity, thus disrupting the environment as little as possible. Initially, the student should be accompanied by a staff person who functions as a trainer/advocate, making introductions, facilitating interaction, and helping the student participate to the maximum extent possible.

Continue Assessment and Intervention.

As integration activities continue, assess the student's strengths and deficits in the new setting and develop strategies for improving weaknesses and accentuating the student's abilities.

Provide Feedback Opportunities.

Make sure that those involved in the integration experience, either directly or peripherally, have a chance to provide feedback and suggestions. To supplement personal contacts and phone conversations, a simple questionnaire can be sent out each month to parents, other teachers, administrators, and to nonhandicapped community leaders and participants.

Monitor and Report Progress.

Periodic progress reports should be sent to related staff persons and/or family members to keep them informed and interested. These reports also help ensure accountability and progress on individual student objectives.

Advertise Programs.

Because the program itself may be unique and innovative, be sure to publicize your activities by inviting community VIP's, parents, and the media to observe, thus fostering support for community integration efforts even in the face of reduced funding.

Provide Reinforcement.

Reward the community for its help, participation, and interest. Giving out certificates of appreciation, writing thank-you notes, or sharing extra snapshots of ongoing activities are examples of rewards that build good will and community support.

INTERVENTION STRATEGIES

Systematic instructional strategies used in a good classroom program can and should be applied in community settings. Community training should *not* be viewed simply as a posttest environment for classroom training, but rather as an arena for continued learning. Techniques such as chaining, fading, prompt hierarchies, simple or complex reinforcement schedules, role-playing, behavioral rehearsal, feedback, and practice are all viable strategies in the community.

Since the ultimate goal of all instruction is to enable the student to respond to natural environmental cues, community trainers must identify and use these cues or prompts throughout the program. After identifying natural cues at work in the environment, apply techniques such as establishing a specific waiting period prior to teacher prompting, systematic pairing and redundant cueing, and reinforcement for self-initiated behaviors. Fortunately, the menu of reinforcers is usually far more varied and powerful in natural settings than in the structured classroom.

The instructional techniques used should actually serve as a model of treatment and a form of advocacy for the student with a severe handicap. The nonhandicapped in the community will undoubtedly view the trainer as an expert and will model his or her approach. Thus, it is important to present age-appropriate techniques, emphasizing understanding and respect for the student as a fellow human being. Preparation through heavy emphasis on simulated practice and role-playing prior to entering the community environment will help students be viewed in a more credible light.

WAYS TO FACILITATE COMMUNITY INTEGRATION

In order to implement the model listed in Figure 1 it will be helpful to review several specific ways to accomplish the integration goals. These ideas are listed below:

1. Facilitate participation in regular recreational groups. It is not necessary to create separate scout troops, Sunday school classes, or bowling teams. Social groups and clubs provide ideal arenas for developing appropriate social interactions. Available groups include: scouts, church groups, adult or child recreation classes, community or neighborhood teams, boys' clubs, and activities at YMCA, YWCA, and similar organizations.
2. Provide community training in stores, services, restaurants, and/or public transportation services. Through community training, persons with severe handicaps can learn to negotiate common aspects of community life, and citizens gain exposure to persons with severe handicaps.
3. Provide appropriate training to enhance recreational integration. Teach persons with handicaps age-appropriate leisure skills to facilitate their ability to use community resources.
4. Provide job training and placement in local business and industry. Persons with severe handicaps need not be relegated to life in adult activity centers or sheltered workshops if appropriate vocational training is started early and continued on a long-term basis.
5. Enable the family to have access to the community with their child. Some families find it very difficult to take their children with handicaps anywhere due to behavior or mobility problems. Often you can offer simple advice or suggestions to improve this situation significantly.

EVALUATION

The effectiveness of the program, regardless of duration, must be evaluated in order to determine whether a given community setting

FIGURE 1
**Steps in Initiating and Implementing
a Community Integration Placement**

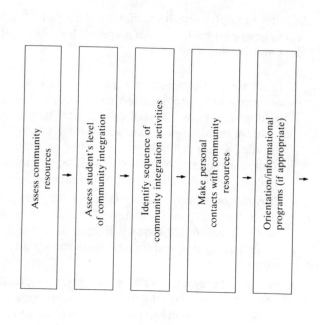

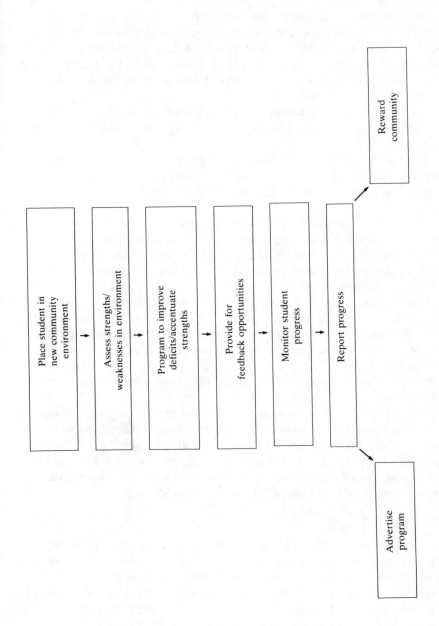

is meeting the needs of the student as well as the nonhandicapped participants. Several specific dimensions can be assessed.

First, monitor the instructional objective originally targeted for completion through direct observation and recording of behaviors. For example, if it was decided that Ron will be taught to order a soda independently at the local ice cream shop, then a post-instructional evaluation should indicate whether he can now perform this skill, and if not, where he is deficient.

Second, code the teacher's level of acceptance for the activity. The teacher's attitude and belief in the value of the program will influence its success.

The social acceptance of the handicapped student by nonhandicapped individuals is perhaps the most important feature of the experience, and should be gauged through anecdotal and formal measures.

Yet another evaluative aspect of the program must be the student's own responses—affective expressions of pleasure and, if possible, verbal statements indicating preference for the activity. A community integration experience which fails to produce a positive response in the student is self-defeating.

Finally, it is crucial to assess parent and family reactions. If there is little interest or if the activity does not generate a positive response from the family, it is unlikely that follow-through and subsequent opportunities to engage in the activity will occur. Parents must be involved and invited to participate in at least the early stages of community integration activities, especially those which occur after school hours.

Taken together, all facets of the evaluation data will help staff make decisions about the selection of future community placement sites. Furthermore, they will provide concrete demonstrations of student competence to parents and other agencies, and will help document the importance of expanding school instructional activities for youths experiencing severe handicaps beyond the classroom setting.

CONCLUSION

This chapter has briefly described goals and strategies for facilitating community integration of students with severe handicaps. There are numerous ways to access home environments, community settings, and leisure programs. In this chapter we have tried to list ideas and resources which might be used. It is important to recognize that school-based programs alone are not sufficient to train students with severe handicaps in appropriate community behaviors. Only community environments will provide this opportunity. The reader interested in additional information about community integration of students with severe handicaps is referred to Brown et al. (1983) and Wehman and Hill (1982).

REFERENCES

Brown, L., Nisbet, J., Ford, A., Sweet, M., Shiraga, B., York, J. & Loomis, R. (1983). The critical need for non-school instruction in educational programs for severely handicapped students. *The Journal of the Association for the Severely Handicapped*, *8*, 71-77.
Wehman, P. & Hill, J. (1982). Preparing severely handicapped youth for less restrictive environments. *The Journal of the Association for the Severely Handicapped*, *7*, 33-39.

Chapter 13

A Summary of Strategies Utilized in Model Programs and Resource Materials

Steven J. Taylor and Dianne Ferguson

In September, 1977, Albuquerque Public Schools closed their only segregated facility for students with severe handicaps. Over 100 children and youths attended regular public schools for the first time. While some parents supported the move, others opposed it fiercely. Many feared that their children would not be safe in regular schools or would receive a substandard education. A parent group formed

Note: This chapter grows out of a national search for promising practices and model programs for integrating students with severe disabilities into normal school and community environments. Information was collected through phone interviews and site visits to 12 school programs during 1981. In all likelihood, many of the programs visited have improved considerably since 1981 and many other programs have been established and nourished throughout the nation. The 12 programs visited included Albuquerque Public Schools; Birmingham Public Schools; Madison Metropolitan School District; Tacoma School District, Jowonio School; Vermont Interdisciplinary Team and selected Vermont school districts; Project A.M.E.S., Ames, Iowa; Project TEACCH and selected school districts, North Carolina; Dekalb County Special Education Association, Illinois; East Central Cooperative Education Program for the Handicapped, Urbana, Illinois; Downeast Project, Bangor, Maine; and Special Help, Portland Public Schools, Maine.

For a general description of the methodology on which these site visits were based, see Bogdan & Taylor, 1975; Special Education Resource Center, 1982, and Taylor, 1982.

Development of this chapter was supported by Contract No. 300-80-0723 with the U.S. Department of Education. The opinions expressed herein are solely those of the authors. The authors would like to thank the many people who contributed to this paper and reviewed earlier drafts. Special thanks to Douglas Biklen, Lu Christie, Alison Ford, Ruth Loomis, Jan Nisbet, Debbie Olson, Stan Searl, and Jo Thomason.

to fight the closing of the segregated school and organized a legal defense fund. By the end of the 1977-78 school year, however, parents originally opposed to the integration program had become supporters. They donated thousands of dollars collected through the defense fund to support integration at the high school.

Such scenes, while not yet commonplace, are occurring with increasing frequency. Entire states (Vermont; Hawaii; and, for autistic students, North Carolina), school districts (Madison, Wisconsin; Albuquerque, New Mexico; Tacoma, Washington; Portland and Bangor, Maine; Birmingham, Alabama; Urbana and DeKalb, Illinois), and individual schools (Jowonio and Ed Smith Schools, Syracuse, New York) are engaged in major integration efforts. At these and other sites, parents, administrators, regular teachers, special educators, and others report that integration is proceeding.

In this chapter, the authors examine model programs throughout the nation and summarize strategies used in the programs to promote integration. Also included is a summary of resource material available to assist in the promotion of integration.

INTEGRATION STRATEGIES

From Vermont to Hawaii, from Wisconsin to New Mexico, from Illinois to Alabama, students with severe disabilities are attending regular schools, interacting with their nonhandicapped peers, and participating in normal community environments. The critical issue facing educators, administrators, and parents is not whether integration can work, but *how* to make it work. As Wilcox and Sailor (1980) state:

> In light of the professional consensus and the various legal and programmatic arguments supporting it, the appropriate question is not, "Should we do it?" or "Does it work?", but rather, "How can we make it work?" Now that the basic criterion has been articulated, it is time to focus, not on further consensus, but on implementation. (p. 282)

In a growing number of schools, districts, and states across the nation, committed educators, working together with parents, university leaders, and others, have developed creative strategies to educate students with severe disabilities in normal school and community settings (Special Education Resource Center, 1982). In this section, the strategies used are summarized. The strategies are discussed under 12 different concerns facing educators when integration occurs.

Dispersal

Albuquerque, Birmingham, Madison, Tacoma, and other districts have closed segregated facilities for the handicapped, while in Vermont and other locations segregated schools are being phased out. The result is that students with severe disabilities are dispersed throughout regular public schools.

Of course, districts vary according to the number of students with severe handicaps at each integrated school. Some districts attempt to adhere to the "principle of natural proportions;" that is, that the proportion of students with severe handicaps at a regular school should approximate their proportion in the school population, approximately 1% (Brown et al., 1977; Wilcox & Sailor, 1980). For example, in Madison, one to five classes are located in each of 11 separate elementary, middle, and high schools. The largest number of students with severe handicaps at any school is 35, out of a population of 2,000. Birmingham's 85 students in the profound mental retardation category are dispersed in 15 classes in nine separate schools. In many rural areas of Vermont and New Hampshire, schools contain a single class of students with severe disabilities.

Other school districts, in contrast, place a relatively large number of classes at each integrated school. While this may help overcome logistical and administrative problems in offering specialized services, it probably limits the degree of social integration at each school. Albuquerque, which terms its program for students with severe handicaps the "Side-by-Side" approach, has eight or more classes for the students with severe handicaps in each of seven regular schools (see Thomason & Arkell, 1980). The number of students with severe disabilities ranges from 60 to 88 in six elementary and middle schools, while the high school serves 134 students with severe handicaps out of a total population of roughly 3,000. However, Albuquerque is in the process of integrating a second high school and an additional elementary school.

A summary of strategies found to be useful in dispersing students with severe handicaps throughout regular schools include the following:

1. Place students as close as possible to the schools they would attend if they were not handicapped.
2. Place students with severe handicaps in age-appropriate schools.
3. Avoid placing students with severe handicaps in schools with a large concentration of other special classes.
4. When starting to integrate, select schools in which principals and other personnel are receptive.
5. Disperse classes for the students with severe handicaps throughout the regular school building and in proximity to classes for nonhandicapped students of the same age. Avoid congregating classes in isolated sections and nonacademic areas.
6. Find alternative uses for segregated facilities. For example, Albuquerque sold its segregated school to a technical vocational institute when it moved to an integrated system.

Many of these strategies have been discussed in more detail in previous chapters of this book.

ITIES FOR INTERACTION

ant that students with severe disabilities be socially in-
h their nondisabled peers. Indeed, a school can hardly
be cul... ed integrated unless students actually interact with one
another. As Stainback, Stainback, and Jaben (1981) note, teachers
should work to structure opportunities for interaction between students
with severe handicaps and nonhandicapped students.

Students with severe disabilities are being involved in a broad
range of extracurricular and nonacademic activities. What follows is
a summary of strategies utilized in model programs throughout the
nation for promoting interactions with typical students. Many of these
strategies have been discussed in detail throughout this book.

1. Arrange for students with severe handicaps to use the cafeteria,
   playground, hallway, lockers, and school buses at the same time as
   other students.
2. Involve the students with severe handicaps in assemblies, social
   activities, and graduation exercises.
3. Schedule joint field trips with regular classes.
4. Arrange for students with severe handicaps to use the school library
   or media center in small groups.
5. Place students with severe handicaps in regular music, art, and
   physical education classes, as well as in homerooms and study halls.
6. Design cooperative work projects between students with severe
   handicaps and nonhandicapped students.
7. Involve typical students in classes for students with severe handicaps. For example, typical students can serve as helpers, buddies,
   and tutors in special classes.
8. Structure joint play sessions between students with severe handicaps and nonhandicapped students during recess.
9. Arrange classroom exchanges between special and regular classes
   for independent seat work, cooking, and nonacademic activities.
10. Assign students with severe handicaps regular school jobs. For
    instance, in Madison and Milwaukee they serve as tardy office
    monitors, attendance monitors, cafeteria helpers, and audio-visual
    equipment aides.

In a small number of schools across the nation, students with
severe handicaps and typical students are learning together in the
same classrooms. Integrated classrooms may be found at Jowonio
(a private school) and Ed Smith (a public school), as well as at
McCollum (Albuquerque) and Blue Mountain (rural Vermont) elementary schools. Jowonio has four integrated classrooms with about 4
autistic and 10 typical children in each class. At Blue Mountain, a 14-
year old girl with severe multiple disabilities is integrated in a regular
class with the support of a full-time aide.

At Jowonio, McCollum, and Blue Mountain, the integrated class-rooms are carefully designed to provide for both interaction between handicapped students and nonhandicapped children and for individual-ized instruction. Each classroom contains a group meeting area and individual learning centers where staff work with children individually or in small groups.

Planning

Integration requires careful planning and preparation (Stetson et al., 1981). Where will classes for the students with severe handicaps be located? How will transportation and related services be provided? How will support from principals, regular and special educators, and parents be obtained? How will negative attitudes be countered? These and other issues must be addressed systematically.

In Madison, Albuquerque, Bangor, Milwaukee, Birmingham, Urbana, and Tacoma schools, integration was preceded by careful plan-ning and preparation (Hamre-Nietupski & Nietupski, 1981; Nietupski, Hamre-Nietupski, Schuetz, & Ockwood, 1980; Stetson et al., 1981; Ritchie, Gruenewald, & Shroeder, 1979).

A summary of strategies used in fostering planning for the integral involvement of students with handicaps in regular school activities include:

1. Create a task force to develop an integration plan. For example, in 1977 Madison formed a Section 504 Task Force to develop a long-term plan for the creation of barrier-free educational settings.
2. Designate a faculty member or consultant to plan for integration.
3. Conduct inservice sessions for regular and special education staff.
4. Arrange visits for special educators to regular schools and regular educators to special schools.
5. Meet with administrators and teachers at the integration site.
6. Arrange for students with severe handicaps to use as many school facilities as possible.
7. Teach students with severe handicaps age-appropriate behavior in regular schools.
8. Involve parents in integration plans.
9. Arrange a faculty "drop-in" to answer questions about integration.
10. Give regular students a day off to visit programs for students experiencing severe handicaps and vice versa.
11. Develop a handbook on integration ideas and activities for teachers.
12. Systematically plan individual student transitions to the next school.

The reader is referred to Chapter 11 for more information about many of the strategies summarized above.

Program Support

Ensuring that teachers and other personnel are well versed in current educational approaches poses a major challenge for any program serving children with severe disabilities. The task of providing program and curriculum support is especially crucial for integrated school systems in which educators are dispersed throughout a number of schools or spread out over a large geographical area.

Vermont's Interdisciplinary Team (I-Team) and North Carolina's Project TEACCH (for autistic children) are two notable statewide program support systems for teachers of students experiencing severe handicaps in dispersed location (Sousie et al., 1978). The Vermont I-Team, established in 1975, provides on-site training, consultation, and assistance to special educators throughout the state to enable children with severe disabilities to be served in regular schools in their home communities. Sponsored by the University of Vermont and funded by the state, the I-Team consists of a core team of professionals–a coordinator, an educational specialist, full- and part-time physical therapists, a part-time occupational therapist, and a communications specialist, in addition to physicians obtained through a subcontract–and four regional educational specialists. I-Team members draw on a range of approaches in working with teachers, including training, individual consultation, critical feedback, and emotional support, as well as developing teaching plans and IEP's, conducting assessments, demonstrating and modeling approaches, writing grant proposals, developing data systems, surveying community resources, and making placement recommendations. During the 1980-81 school year, the I-Team served 164 students directly.

In Madison and other districts, program support teachers assist and consult with special educators on a district level. The Madison school district employs 18 program support teachers, four of whom are responsible for students labeled severely retarded. In addition to working with individual special educators, the program support teachers provide inservice training to regular education staff and play a liaison role with parents and community agencies. As mandated by school district policy and the contract with the teachers' union, program support teachers are not involved in teacher evaluation and supervision.

Other support strategies implemented in Madison include an extensive staff development and inservice training program, informal monthly meetings between the program coordinator and special education personnel, task forces in curriculum development staffed by teachers and advanced graduate students from the University of Wisconsin at Madison, and development of instructional manuals by the school district and university.

In Albuquerque, an assistant principal is assigned to each Side-by-Side school to coordinate the program for students with severe handicaps. Certified in special education, the assistant principals, who report to building principals, perform a variety of functions: staff evaluation, scheduling, monitoring programs, curriculum consultation, interviewing prospective staff, conducting team meetings, liaison with parents, and coordination of IEP development and implementation. They not only support educational staff, but also relieve building principals of many responsibilities associated with special education and thus head off potential backlash to serving children with severe disabilities at regular schools.

Specialized Services

Special education and related services traditionally have been organized according to what Thomason and Arkell (1980) term "a cluster approach." Services such as special education, physical therapy, occupational therapy, communications training, and vocational training have been offered at a centralized location. Integration requires a decentralization of specialized services.

At integrated schools, related services can be provided for either by building-based or itinerant specialists. Each Albuquerque Side-by-Side school is staffed by a full set of related-services professionals. The Madison school district assigns physical therapists, occupational therapists, and speech and language specialists to one to three schools, depending on the total school population in need of these services. They serve as consultants to clasroom teachers as well as providing direct services to students. In rural Vermont, itinerant I-Team professionals consult with classroom teachers on related services on-site. Regional educational specialists offer ongoing support to teachers on related services approaches.

Supporting Regular Teachers

A frequent criticism of integration is that it places undue demands on regular teachers. If students with severe handicaps are to be fully integrated into school activities, schools must provide incentives for regular teachers to be involved with them. At Albuquerque's McCollum School, the principal and assistant principal support regular teachers serving children with severe disabilities in many ways. A summary of strategies for supporting regular teachers in their integration efforts include:

1. Aides from special classes are assigned to assist regular teachers when students with severe handicaps attend physical education classes and extracurricular activities.
2. Regular teachers are relieved of paperwork responsibilities for students with severe handicaps. While they are invited to attend IEP conferences, it is not required.
3. Regular teachers share many special education resources, including materials and aides to run dittos and perform other tasks.
4. Regular students are included in field trips, picnics, and other activities for Side-by-Side students.
5. Special education teachers consult with regular teachers on educational approaches and offer remedial help to individual students.

A potential incentive for regular teachers to integrate is reducing class size in return for accepting a student experiencing a severe handicap into the regular classroom.

Community Integration

In accordance with increased acceptance of the importance of teaching students with severe handicaps functional life skills, a growing number of school programs use normal community environments as training sites. Students with severe disabilities interact with regular workers, bus drivers, shopkeepers, clerks, waiters, and other members of the public in the course of the school day.

In Madison, Dekalb, Urbana, and Ames, small groups (one to five) of students with severe handicaps are taught functional skills in shopping centers, parks, grocery stores, domestic environments (a teacher's or aide's home), and work settings. Madison schools have 80 community job sites available while Project A.M.E.S. utilizes 13 separate work training settings. Job sites include hospitals, motels, labs, human services agencies, churches, factories, insurance companies, and university offices. Secondary-age students may spend as much as 75% of the school day outside of school buildings.

Project A.M.E.S. and the Madison, Urbana, and Dekalb programs employ community vocational teachers or consultants to coordinate community vocational training efforts. For instance, Madison has 5 1/2 community vocational teachers. While vocational teachers assume primary responsibility for training students, classroom teachers and aides may be involved in actual training and supervision.

Community vocational teachers perform many functions: recruiting job sites, performing ecological inventories prior to student placement, student training and supervision, and quality control—a key factor in winning over prospective employers and in troubleshooting. For example, they might meet with union officials at work sites to gain support and allay fears.

The Madison school district also employs a full-time transition specialist to place graduates of the programs for students with severe handicaps in regular jobs. In addition to working directly with students and employers, the transition specialist assists and consults with parents and other agencies in planning students' postschool careers. Since 1979, 27 of the 38 graduates of the severely handicapped program have been placed in integrated vocational environments (Brown et al., 1983).

Integrating the Staff

If children are to be integrated, staff must be also. Integration calls for cooperation and support of all school staff. Regular educators and other personnel must be willing to counter negative attitudes among typical children, plan joint activities with special educators, and encourage positive interactions between students with severe handicaps and nonhandicapped students.

A summary of strategies for integrating special and regular education staff members include:

1. Have one staff lounge for special and regular teachers.
2. Conduct joint staff meetings and inservice training sessions, including sessions on integration approaches and special education issues.
3. Assign special education teachers as coaches of athletic teams and sponsors of student service groups and extracurricular activities. In Tacoma, special education teachers are responsible for one extracurricular non-special education activity.
4. Arrange informal meetings and social activities to encourage staff communication and cohesiveness. One principal in Urbana schedules informal get-togethers for all school staff, including cafeteria workers, secretaries, and custodians.
5. Demonstrate administrative support for integration. At Price Elementary School in Birmingham, the principal serves as a model for regular education staff by visiting special education classes regularly, interacting with students with severe handicaps on playgrounds, eating lunch with students with severe handicaps, and building materials for special classes.

Some of these strategies were discussed in more detail in Chapter 11.

Parental Support

Parental acceptance and involvement are critical elements in the success of integration efforts (Stetson et al., 1981). While some parental fears of integration are to be expected, many of these will dissipate as quality integrated programs are implemented.

Parental support for integration can be gained through carefully planned strategies. A summary of strategies designed to foster parental support of integration, that have been used in Albuquerque, Madison, and Birmingham include:

1. Arrange parent visits to regular schools prior to integration.
2. Make presentations at parent groups.
3. Include parents in planning task forces.
4. Invite parents to volunteer in classrooms or help out on integrated field trips.
5. Encourage parents of students with severe handicaps to join and participate in the regular parent-teacher organization.
6. Describe and promote integration efforts in school newsletters and annual reports.

ATTITUDES

Perhaps the best way to counter negative attitudes toward the disabled held by typical children is through sustained interaction. Typical children can hardly learn to understand and accept their peers who experience severe handicaps if they are not exposed to them. Research on the subject presents conflicting findings. Some researchers report an increase in negative attitudes among nonhandicapped children after contact with the students with handicaps (Gottlieb & Budoff, 1973; Gottlieb & Davis, 1973). However, a growing body of research demonstrates increased acceptance and understanding of students with severe handicaps on the part of typical children as a result of integration (McHale & Simeonsson, 1980; Stainback & Stainback, 1981; Voeltz, 1980, 1982). In any case, it is obvious that integration efforts should be accompanied by systematic strategies to foster positive attitudes among the nonhandicapped toward children with severe disabilities (Stainback et al., 1981).

A summary of strategies that have been employed to foster positive attitudes among students toward their peers who experience severe handicaps include:

1. Conduct sensitization sessions with the use of books, films, and filmstrips., Extensive attitude-change curricula already exist (Barnes, Berrigan, & Biklen, 1978; Biklen & Bogdan, 1976; Biklen & Sokoloff, 1978; Bookbinder, 1978; Cohen, 1977; Sarson, Brightman, & Blatt, 1978).
2. Incorporate sessions on human differences into social studies, health, English, human relations, and other classes (Nietupski et al., 1980).
3. Teach typical children signs and symbols (e.g., Blissymbolics) to enable them to communicate with children with severe handicaps who use these alternative communication systems.
4. Design group exercises to teach the nonhandicapped what they have in common with students with severe disabilities. Jowonio teachers ask all children to identify their own and others' strengths and weaknesses, while a kindergarten teacher in Birmingham asks her children to think of ways they are like students with severe handicaps in the class next door.
5. Invite an adult with disabilities to speak to regular classes.

Tutors, Helpers, and Buddies

The peer utilization strategies discussed in this book have been implemented in many school districts. At integrated schools across the country, typical students serve as tutors, helpers, and friends for their severely handicapped peers (Almond, Rodgers, & Krug, 1979). For example, they are involved in activities like escorting students with severe handicaps to the cafeteria, playground, or library, pushing their wheelchairs, playing games with them, accompanying them on field trips, helping them eat or put on coats and hats, and working with them on specific skills. Some school systems have developed extensive buddy programs (Voeltz, Kishi, Brown, & Kube, 1980). In Tacoma, one or more regular students are assigned to each student experiencing a handicap. These "buddies" receive social studies or health credits for the experience and are provided with training and supervision. During the first year of involvement, they serve as "student assistants" before becoming full-fledged "buddies" in their second year. In some instances, student groups have initiated support programs for their peers with severe disabilities, as in the case of Los Compadres at Albuquerque's Manzano High school.

Policies and Procedures

In many school districts, administrative support for integration is expressed in written policies which exceed the broad mandates contained in state and federal laws (Stetson et al., 1981). For instance, the Madison school district's philosophy endorses integration in the regular education program for all students, placement in chronological age-appropriate environments geographically distributed through the district, and nonsegregated service delivery models.

Madison has also developed clearcut mechanisms and policies to support its dynamic, community-referenced educational approach, including budget line items for staff and student transportation to community training sites, and policies covering liability for students placed in community settings, teacher responsibility for supervising aides and student teachers in nonschool environments, use of private residences for training, procedures for planning instructional travel, and other issues.

RESOURCES

Fortunately, finding resources to facilitate integration of students experiencing severe handicaps is becoming much less difficult. The choices are growing at such a rate that we make no attempt to be exhaustive. We have attempted to include some of the resource materials we think teachers will find most useful.[*]

The resource materials included in this section can be used to accomplish a number of the tasks facing educators when integration occurs, such as integrating "special" and "regular" education programs as well as teachers, parents, and students.

Integrating Programs

As has been noted, integration occurs in various ways. Whether formal or informal, in a single class or throughout a district or state—at

---

[*] Our resource selections are loosely based on one or more of the following criteria:(a) The item provides sound, useful information that genuinely supports integration of severely handicapped students into public school and community settings; (b) the item itself contains further resources, such as bibliographies, lists of materials, addresses of media distributors, parent organizations, or advocacy groups, etc; (c) the item is recent and/or likely to be fairly easily accessible.

some point the commitment to integrate must become widely shared. All the people involved with schools—regular and special educators, staff, administrators, parents, and students—need to understand and be prepared for integration. While some successful early efforts were serendipitous, careful planning and preparation ensure a more certain outcome.

The Complete School: Integrating Special and Regular Education (Biklen, in press) is a comprehensive book about how special and regular education programs can be integrated. The contributing authors (Douglas Biklen, Robert Bogdan, Stan Searl, Dianne Ferguson, Steven Taylor) spent literally hundreds of hours in real school situations observing integration in action. They also interviewed teachers, administrators, parents, and students to find out what they thought about integration. The results of their work provide fresh insights about integration. The findings also provide clear cues as to how many of the difficulties associated with integration can be overcome with little real expense to school districts.

"Preparing School Systems for Longitudinal Integration Efforts" (Hamre-Nietupski, Nietupski, Stainback & Stainback, 1984) and "Facilitating Integration through Personnel Preparation" (Stainback & Stainback, 1984), both chapters in *Public School Integration of Severely Handicapped Students* (Certo, Haring & York, 1984), review two arenas for assisting the integration of special education programs into regular education: inservice and preservice training. The first reviews strategies for preparing and involving school staff and assessing and evaluating a district-wide integration effort. Also included are two checklists and discussion of one inventory for evaluating attitudes among students and staff toward the severely handicapped, and the "integration status" of the school itself. The second chapter discusses the implications of integration for personnel preparation. Changes in the preparation of both special and regular educators are suggested. In addition, the authors suggest a need to direct more serious efforts to preparing the wider society for lifelong integration of people with severe handicaps through education and support of other service providers, families, and the general public.

Attitudes and Inservice Manual (A.I.M.) (Murray, Beckstead, & Sailor, in preparation) is an example of an inservice program aimed largely at regular educators and students. Its goal is to train school and community personnel to implement an on-going project that: (a) provides information about students with severe disabilities; (b) plans interactions between students; and (c) changes both attitudes and behaviors toward students experiencing severe handicaps. Enclosed is an extensive bibliography of books, articles, and audio-visual materials organized by ages from preschool through adult.

Equal in importance to the preparation of regular educators is that of special educators. Integration has extensive implications for educational content of programs for students with severe handicaps. In fact, traditional educational models and practices may conflict both philosophically and pragmatically with integration. *A Series of*

Professional Training Modules on the Education of Severely Handicapped Learners: An Update on Educational Best Practices (Voeltz, 1983) addresses just this problem. It pulls together material in four areas of curricular and instructional innovation: (a) teaching functional skills using natural environments; (b) instructional technology that facilitates skill acquisition; (c) individualized curriculum sequencing; and (d) issues related to programs for secondary students (see next section for more specific resources on these topics).

Severely Handicapped Students in Regular Schools: A Progress Report (Nietupski et al, 1980) reports on a successful district-wide integration effort in Milwaukee. The project focused on integrating secondary students, though some efforts were made to expand the project to some elementary sites. The authors discuss the formal and informal strategies used to prepare and facilitate involvement and interaction among regular education staff, nonhandicapped students, and the handicapped students themselves. The report also includes a list of resources including books, movies, films and slides, all designed to sensitize students to their peers experiencing handicaps.

Finally, *Teaching and Mainstreaming Autistic Children* (Knoblock, 1982) reports another successful total program integration effort, albeit on a smaller scale than a school district, this one directed to early childhood programs. The author discusses preschool and primary integrated programs, different curricular approaches, integration of families and schools, and strategies for promoting positive attitudes and relationships among all school participants. The book is largely a report of Jowonio: The Learning Place, a private integrated school in Syracuse, New York, and is written primarily by the school's staff.

Integrating Students

The distinction we've made here between integrating programs and integrating students is an arbitrary one. All of the items mentioned above include considerations, strategies, and ideas designed to facilitate positive interactions between disabled and nondisabled students. After all, it's not just that people with severe handicaps have a right not to be segregated; all students have a right to learn about, from, and with as wide a variety of peers as possible. The items in this section focus directly on students and how to prepare them to understand and appreciate even very dramatic differences in people.

What's the Difference? (Barnes et al., 1978) is written for teachers about how to accomplish a first step: "teaching positive attitudes toward people with disabilities." After some general introductory sections examining values and myths about disabilities and disabled people, the bulk of the book contains activities and ideas for use in classrooms. Using a lesson plan-like format, activities and lessons relating to a wide range of disabilities (motor impairment, mental retardation, emotional disturbance, and health impairment among others) and employing a variety of lesson formats (e.g., group discussion, individual paper and pencil work simulations, speakers, interviewing, etc.) are included. All the activities are designed to meet one or more of the following goals: (a) provide information about disabilities; (b) increase comfortableness with people who experience disabilities; (c) foster empathy; and (d) encourage accepting behavior toward people with disabilities. Also included is an annotated reference section listing general books, articles, journals, children's books, films, and slides, directed to students and adults and encompassing a wide variety of disabilities.

In a similar vein, "Program and Curriculum Innovations to Prepare Children for Integration" (Voeltz, 1984) reports on the specific strategies with curricular/instructional changes made as part of the Hawaii Integration Project. The Project developed specific modifications to the existing regular education curriculum, and implemented two new curriculum components. A "social performance" component was directed to the preparation of students with severe handicaps for integrated settings. The other curriculum component, the Special Friends Program, is "a systematic, structured, peer interaction program." Although the Special Friends Program is discussed in this chapter, a more detailed description is also available in a new revised trainers manual (Voeltz et al., 1983).

Integrating Instruction

Having arrived in public school, satisfied the caution and curiosity of regular staff and peers, there still remains the challenge of determining what and how to teach students with severe disabilities. Much is available in this area, and we will only highlight a few key examples and themes.

An important foundation of integration and all its implications for schools and teaching is the principle of normalization. *Normalization, Social Integration, and Community Services* (Flynn & Nitsch, 1980) provides a broad introduction to normalization. It includes the earliest Scandinavian formulations by Bank-Mikkelsen and Nirje as well as Wolfensberger's succinct description: Normalization refers to the use of culturally valued means in order to enable people to live culturally valued lives. In addition, Wolfensberger discusses issues surrounding a variety of misconceptions of normalization and the implications of the principle for empirical research. Although this book's discussion of normalization focuses more on community service alternatives than schools, much of the discussion and many of the examples can easily be understood from a schooling perspective.

A key formulation of the instructional implications of normalization and integration is the "Criterion of Ultimate Functioning" (Brown, Nietupski, & Hamre-Nietupski, 1976), first discussed in a chapter of *Hey! Don't Forget About Me* (Thomas, 1976). Central to the concept is the recognition that if people with severe handicaps are to be integrated, both during the schooling years and in adult life, then many familiar instructional practices—such as one-to-one instruction, repeated practice, and simulated learning environments—will have to be altered. Brown and his colleagues outline some of these in his article, especially teaching "functional skills" in "natural environments."

Much of the work done by this particular group has been published in various forms in a variety of books and articles. However, through a collaboration with the Madison Metropolitan School District, they have produced a series of "curriculum books." (Information is available from Dr. Lee Gruenewald, Director, Department of Specialized Educational Services, Madison Metropolitan School District, 545 W. Dayton Street, Madison WI 53703.) Volume VIII (1978), for example, includes a key article on how to devise "chronologically age-appropriate and functional curricular content" for secondary school students. This same volume also contains articles on curricular strategies for developing interactions between students with severe handicaps and nonhandicapped students, and the use of naturally occurring cues and correction procedures. Volume X (1980) includes a key article on the notions of "partial participation" and "individualized adaptations."

Educational Programming for the Severely and Profoundly Handicapped (Sontag, Smith & Certo 1977), while an early effort, continues to be a comprehensive examination of education for students with severe handicaps. It includes policy statements on "community reintegration," problems and solutions for providing services, including such cases as services in rural areas, and services for infants and preschoolers as well as adults. Also included is an examination of teaching strategies in a number of different areas.

Two more recent books focus in more detail on instructional issues and techniques. *Methods of Instruction for Severely Handicapped Students* (Sailor, Wilcox, & Brown, 1980) focuses in several chapters on making decisions about what to teach, especially Chapter 3 on teaching language and Chapter 10 on teaching to the "next environment" in preschool programs. *Severely Handicapped Students: An Instructional Design* (Sailor & Guess, 1983) is a textbook which offers a comprehensive system that may serve as a basis for organizing instructional programs for students with severe handicaps. Much of the focus here is on selecting, sequencing, and evaluating curriculum content. The authors introduce a strategy called the "functional curriculum-sequencing model" which features the teaching of functional skill clusters that are naturally sequenced according to the students' own environments.

Finally, we include three very different books. *Design of High School Programs for Severely Handicapped Students* (Wilcox & Bellamy, 1982) discusses the challenges unique to programs for older students. Who decides what to teach and why? How do schools provide effective transitions for students to adult services and environments? And what impact do such issues have on both the instructional control and strategy? Focusing more exclusively on early childhood, *Teach and Reach* (Barnes, Eyman, & Bragar, 1977) is a collection of ideas, activities, and resources for both special and regular education teachers. The book is based on the authors' experiences as teachers in an alternative program that integrated all "levels" of children with handicaps and nonhandicapped children in the same class. Thus, the book addresses teaching *all* children, not just children with severe handicaps and on helping teachers independently implement new, creative ideas, since "schools change because people in them change." *Mealtimes for Severely*

Retarded and Profoundly Handicapped Persons (Perske, Clifton, McLean & Stein, 1977) is a unique book. It brings together a wide variety of people including parents, people with handicaps, volunteers, therapists, and teachers to discuss issues surrounding mealtimes. It begins with the notion that mealtimes for people with severe handicaps can be valuable learning experiences. To this end, the book includes a lot of specific information on techniques, equipment, and other new and developing technologies. The book also moves well beyond this to present the perspective that mealtimes are as valuable for how children mature socially as well as physically. Sections on "creative interactions," "helpful settings," and "creative uses of people" all include insightful and sensitive articles illustrating this value perspective. Also included is a well-annotated bibliography of resources.

Integrating Parents

At one program the teachers were frightened by the emotional intensity of a mother's reaction to seeing her daughter with a severe handicap having lunch with the fourth and fifth graders. The mother's explanation—that her reaction arose from witnessing the integration that had always seemed an impossible hope—only further confused the teachers. They had concluded the mother was "not ready" to see her daughter in such extreme contrast to nonhandicapped peers, that she needed time to "adjust" and "accept" the integrated program.

Whether a parent is a long-term advocate or new to integration, the actual event can produce strong reactions—even confusion, uncertainty, or fear. In addition to emphasizing the kind of strategies mentioned above, teachers can assist parental integration by: (a) listening carefully to parents in order to understand their experiences; and (b) helping parents to empower themselves.

Hope for the Families (Perske, 1981) is an excellent example of understanding acquired through listening. Although the book is written for parents, teachers can acquire a quick introduction to some of the important feelings, conflicts and strategies families use as they integrate children with handicaps into their families. The book is sensitive, well-written, and interestingly illustrated.

Parents themselves often speak most eloquently, and published parent narratives constitute an excellent source for teachers and other professionals. *Parents Speak Out* (Turnbull & Turnbull, 1978) subtitled "Views From the Other Side of the Two-Way Mirror" contains 14 separate accounts of parents who are also professionals in special education and related fields. Many of the accounts focus on parents' frustration and failure in trying to locate adequate health, education, and social services in spite of the skills and resources afforded by their professional status.

A Difference in the Family (Featherstone, 1980) and *Sticks and Stones* (Pieper, 1977) are both personal accounts of life with a child experiencing a severe disability. Featherstone recounts her experiences as she gradually learned that her son was multiply handicapped and the process by which her family "knit" Jody "and our new identities as mother, father, and sisters of a severely handicapped child, into the fabric of an on-going life" (p.5).

In addition, she moves beyond her own personal account to those of others in order to make sense of "the differences in families" in some particularly useful conceptual ways. For example, what many professionals perceive variously as "role conflict," "psychological stress," "hostility," or "guilt," Featherstone discusses in terms of "loneliness" and "fatigue."

Pieper's account in *Sticks and Stones* focuses less on personal and family dynamics and more on social criticism and advocacy. She is often angry: angry at the treatment received from doctors, "...everyone admitted that you do not speak up to doctors, and you do not rat on the staff. They have access to your children. We were all so afraid"; angry that there were no "public or private schools in our county that will take Jeff." At the same time, she understands the impact of cultural attitudes, bureaucratic barriers, and historical conventions, and she actively seeks "new ways of organizing and advocating between professionals and consumers."

Although there are many more parent narratives, *Does She Know She's There?* (Schaefer, 1982) and *The Seige* (Park, 1982) are both now available in second editions that contain updates. Both Schaefer's daugher, Catherine and Park's, Jessy, are now in their twenties. Catherine, who is multiply handicapped, is beginning a newly developed program at the University of Winnipeg and plans to move to an apartment. Jessy, who is autistic, works part time in a college mailroom, earning and saving her income to spend on supporting her own needs and interests. With the second editions, these books now reflect the outcomes of struggle—the changes in the families, the services and the hope.

Often a first step is helping to empower parents involved, assisting them to understand and help their own children more effectively and independently. *Steps to Independence* (Baker, Brightman, Heifetz, & Murphy, 1976) is a series of manuals designed to teach parents basic behavioral skills and techniques. There are a total of 10 manuals, including: "Teaching Early (and Advanced) Language Skills;" "Managing Behavior Problems;" "Independent Living;" "Toileting;" and "Play Skills." The text is written simply, but without condescension, and is punctuated by illustrations and short practice tasks. Some of the series is now available in French translation.

There is much talk of "parent involvement" or "parent participation in their child's educational program." *Unraveling the Special Education Maze* (Culter, 1981) takes as its task helping parents understand and exercise their rights with schools. Subtitled "An Action Guide," the book includes a wealth of practical strategies and skills that parents can use to effectively interact with the people, papers, and situations they encounter in schools. Culter includes a particularly effective section on understanding and managing common myths about parents, educators, and children with handicaps. Her parental perspective is strong and helpful throughout.

Having developed social advocacy skills, parents often expand their power base and impact by joining with other parents and supporters. *Let Our Children Go* (Biklen, 1974) is "An Organizing Manual for Advocates and Parents" that includes strategies and examples of how to develop alliances, identify broad community needs, and assess and overcome barriers to change. It also includes a resource section listing books, articles, films and organizations related to organizing, legal rights, integration, and alternatives.

As we said at the beginning of this section, our suggested resources represent a *selected* few of a growing group of high-quality materials concerning integration of students with severe disabilities into public school and community settings. Each of the items we mention contain further resources that if explored will lead the reader into an expanding network of creative, useful material. We encourage teachers to follow these paths.

CONCLUSION

Integrating students with handicaps in regular school programs requires careful planning and preparation, strategies for providing teachers and other school staff with up-to-date information and resources, creation of specialized support positions, development of facilitative policies, and other carefully planned strategies. Yet it would be misleading to portray integration as a simple technical matter. What distinguishes the programs described in this book is a strong belief in the value of educating children with severe disabilities alongside their typical peers and preparing them to participate fully in community life.

Integration works when people are committed to it. Educating children with severe disabilities in regular schools and classrooms is not always easy; it requires creativity and hard work. Yet committed administrators, parents, educators, specialists, and university consultants create ways to make integration successful (see Nietupski et al., 1980). As an Albuquerque teacher explained, "You have to have a belief in it. If you don't want it to work, it won't." A Vermont principal expressed the sentiment: "I don't think any school has an excuse not to do it."

In summary, regular students *can* learn to accept and value their peers who experience disabilities. Parental resistance to integration *can* be overcome. Regular teachers and administrators *can* learn to accomodate students with severe disabilities into their program. Integration *can* work.

REFERENCES

Almond, P., Rodgers, S., & Krug, D. (1979). Mainstreaming: A model for including elementary students in the severely handicapped classroom. *Teaching Exceptional Children, 11*, 135-139.

Baker, B. L., Brightman, A. J., Heifetz, L. J., & Murphy, D. M. (1976). *Steps to independence: A skills training series for children with special needs.* Champaign IL: Research Press.

Barnes, E., Berrigan, C., & Biklen, D. (1978). *What's the difference: Teaching positive attitudes toward people with disabilities.* Syracuse NY: Human Policy Press.

Barnes, E., Eyman, B., & Brager, M. (1977). *Teach and reach: An alternative guide to resources in the classroom.* Syracuse NY: Human Policy Press.

Biklen, D. (in press). *The complete school: Integrating special and regular education.* New York: Teacher's College Press.

Biklen, D. (1974). *Let our children go: An organizing manual for advocates and parents.* Syracuse NY: Human Policy Press.

Biklen, D., & Bogdan, R. (1976). *Handicapism* [Slideshow]. Syracuse, NY: Human Policy Press.

Biklen, D., & Sokoloff, M. (1978). *What do you do when your wheelchair gets a flat tire?* New York: Scholastic Magazine, Inc.

Bogdan, R., & Taylor, S. (1975). *Introduction to qualitative research methods.* New York: John Wiley.

Bookbinder, S. R. (1978). *Meeting street school curriculum.* Boston: Exceptional Parent Press.

Brown, L., Nietupski, J., & Hamre-Nietupski, S. (1976). Criterion of ultimate functioning. In M. A. Thomas (Ed.), *Hey! Don't forget about me* (pp. 2-15). Reston, VA: Council for Exceptional Children, 2-15.

Brown, L., Shiraga, B., Ford, A., Nisbet, J., VanDeventer, P., Sweet, M., & Loomis, R., (1983). *Teaching severely handicapped students to perform meaningful work in nonsheltered vocational environments.* Madison: University of Wisconsin and Madison Metropolitan Public Schools.

Brown, L., Wilcox, B., Sontag, E., Vincent, B., Dodd, N., & Gruenewald, L. (1977). Toward the realization of the least restrictive educational environments for severely handicapped students. *AAESPH Review*, 2, 195-201.

Certo, N., Haring, N., & York, R. (Eds.), (1984). *Public School integration of severely handicapped students.* Baltimore: Paul H. Brookes.

Cohen, S. *Accepting individual differences.* (1977). Niles, IL: Developmental Learning Materials.

Culter, B. C. (1981). *Unraveling the special education maze: An action guide for parents.* Champaign, IL: Research Press.

Featherstone, H. (1980). *A difference in the family: Life with a disabled child.* New York: Basic Books.

Flynn, R., & Nitsch, K. (Eds.). (1980). *Normalization, social integration, and community services.* Baltimore, MD: University Park Press.

Gottlieb, J., & Budoff, M. (1973). Social acceptability of retarded children in nongraded schools differing in architecture. *American Journal of Mental Deficiency*, 78, 15-19.

Gottlieb, J., & Davis, J. E. (1973). Social acceptance of EMRs during overt behavioral interaction. *American Journal of Mental Deficiency*, 78, 141-143.

Hamre-Nietupski, S., & Nietupski, J. (1981). Integral involvement of severely handicapped students within regular public schools. *Journal of the Association for the Severely Handicapped*, 6(2), 30-39.

Hamre-Nietupski, S., Nietupski, J., Stainback, W., & Stainback, S. (1984). Preparing school systems for longitudinal integration efforts. In N. Certo, N. Haring, & R. York (Eds.), *Public school integration of severely handicapped students.* Baltimore: Paul H. Brookes.

Knoblock, P. (1982). *Teaching and mainstreaming autistic children.* Denver, CO: Love Publishing Co.

McHale, S. M., & Simeonsson, R. J. (1980). Effects of interaction on nonhandicapped children's attitudes toward autistic children. *American Journal of Mental Deficiency*, *85*, 18-24

Murray, C., Beckstead, S. P., & Sailor, W. (in preparation). *Attitudes and inservice manual (A.I.M.)*. San Francisco, CA: Project REACH.

Nietupski, J., Hamre-Nietupski, S., Schuetz, G., & Ockwood, L. (1980). *Severely handicapped students in regular schools: A progress report: Milwaukee Public Schools integration efforts*. Milwaukee: Milwaukee Public Schools.

Park, C. C. (1982). *The siege*. Boston, MA: Little, Brown & Co.

Perske, R., Clifton, A., McLean, B. M., & Stein, J. I. (1977). *Mealtimes for severely retarded and profoundly handicapped persons*. Baltimore: University Park Press.

Perske, R. (1981). *Hope for the families*. Nashville, TN: Abingdon Press.

Pieper, E. (1977). *Sticks and stones*. Syracuse, NY: Human Policy Press.

Ritchie, D. S., Gruenewald, L. J., & Schroeder, J. (1979, November). *Integration of moderately and severely handicapped students in public schools*. Paper presented at the Organization for Cooperation and Development, Paris.

Sailor, W., & Guess, D. (1983). *Severely handicapped students: An instructional design*. Boston, MA: Houghton Mifflin Co.

Sailor, W., Wilcox, B., & Brown, L. (Eds.). (1980). *Methods of instruction for severely handicapped students*. Baltimore: Paul H. Brookes.

Sarson, C., Brightman, A., & Blatt, J. (1978). *Feeling free* [films]. New York: Scholastic Magazine, Inc.

Schaefer, N. (1982). *Does she know she's there?* Winnipeg: Fitzhenry & Whiteside.

Sontag, E., Smith, J., & Certo, N. (Eds.). (1977). *Educational programming for the severely and profoundly handicapped*. Reston, VA: Council for Exceptional Children.

Sousie, S., Edelman, S., Christie, L., Fox, T., Fox, W., Hill, M., Williams, W., & York, R. (197). *Providing interdisciplinary support to teachers in rural settings*. Burlington, VT: Center for Developmental Disabilities, University of Vermont.

Special Education Resource Center. (1982). *Special populations: Compendium of practices*. Syracuse, NY: Special Education Resource Center, Syracuse University.

Stainback, W., & Stainback, S. (1981). A review of research on interactions between severely handicapped and non-handicapped students. *Journal of the Association for the Severely Handicapped*, *6*(3), 23-29.

Stainback, W., & Stainback, S. (1984). Facilitating integration through personnel preparation. In N. Certo, N. Haring, & R. York (Eds.), *Public school integration of severely handicapped students*. Baltimore: Paul H. Brookes, 143-154.

Stainback, W., Stainback, S., & Jaben, T. (1981). Providing opportunities for interaction between severely handicapped and non-handicapped students. *Teaching Exceptional Children*, *13*, 72-75.

Stetson, F. E., Elting, S. E., Biggs, L. K., Raimondi, S. L., Burnette, J., & Scheffter, A. (1981). *Options: A training program to present administrative options for implementing the least restrictive environment (LRE) mandate*. Annandale, VA: JWK International Corporation.

Taylor, S. J. (1982). From segregation to integration: Strategies for integrating severely handicapped students in normal school and community settings. *Journal of the Association for the Severely Handicapped, 8,* 42-49.

Thomas, M. A. (Ed.). (1976). *Hey! Don't forget about me.* Reston, VA: Council for Exceptional Children.

Thomason, J., & Arkell, C. (1980). Educating the severely/profoundly handicapped in the public schools: A side-by-side approach. *Exceptional Children, 47,* 114-122.

Turnbull, A. P., & Turnbull, H. R. (1978). *Parents speak out.* Columbus, OH: Charles G. Merrill.

Voeltz, L. (Ed.). (1983). *A series of professional training modules on the education of severely handicapped learners: An update on educational best practices.* Minneapolis, MN: Upper Midwest Regional Resource Center.

Voeltz, L. M. (1980). Children's attitudes toward handicapped peers. *American Journal of Mental Deficiency, 84,* 455-464.

Voeltz, L. M. (1982). Effects of structured interactions with severely handicapped peers on children's attitudes. *American Journal of Mental Deficiency,* 86, 380-390.

Voeltz, L. (1984). Program and curriculum innovations to prepare children for integration. In N. Certo, N. Haring, & R. York (Eds.), *Public school integration of severely handicapped students.* Baltimore: Paul H. Brookes, 155-184.

Voeltz, L. M., Hempill, N. J., Brown, S., Kishi, G., Klein, R., Fruehling, R., Collie, J., Levy, G., & Kube, C. (1983). *The special friends program: A trainer's manual for integrated school settings* (rev. ed.). Honolulu: University of Hawaii Department of Special Education.

Voeltz, L., Kishi, G., Brown, S., & Kube, C. (1980). *Special friends training manual: Starting a project in your school.* Honolulu: University of Hawaii.

Wilcox, B., & Bellamy, G. T. (1982). *Design of high school programs for severely handicapped students.* Baltimore: Paul H. Brookes.

Wilcox, B., & Sailor, W. (1980). Service delivery issues: Integrated educational systems. In B. Wilcox & R. York (Eds.), *Quality education for the severely handicapped: The federal investment.* Washington, DC: U.S. Department of Education, 277-304.

Wilcox, B., & York, R. (Eds.). (1980). *Quality education for the severely handicapped: The federal investment.* Washington, DC: U.S. Department of Education.

Williams, W., & Fox, T. (Eds.). (1977). *Minimum objective system for pupils with severe handicaps.* Burlington, VT: Center for Developmental Disabilities, University of Vermont.